The

Beautiful
Wisdom

Bible Promise
Book®

Hundreds of Scriptures
for a New Life

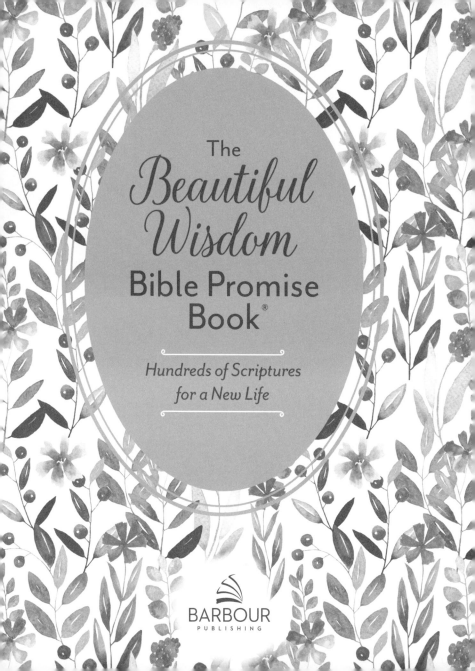

BARBOUR
PUBLISHING

© 2022 by Barbour Publishing, Inc.

Chapter introductions written by Tina Krause.

ISBN 978-1-63609-294-2

Published by Barbour Publishing, Inc., 1810 Barbour Drive, Uhrichsville, Ohio 44683
www.barbourbooks.com

Our mission is to inspire the world with the life-changing message of the Bible.

 Member of the
Evangelical Christian
Publishers Association

Printed in China.

Contents

Introduction

Our world sends many conflicting signals on the important issues of life. How should we approach anger? Is discipline a good thing or not? Why speak with honesty? Is prayer for real? What is true wisdom?

In His kindness, God has answered all of these questions—and many more—in the pages of His Word, the Bible. Whatever our needs, we can find in scripture the principles we need to address the issues we face.

This collection of Bible verses is a handy reference to some of the key issues that all people—and especially women—face. In these pages, you'll find carefully selected verses that address topics like comfort, encouragement, friendship, purity, rest, and understanding. In fact, more than five dozen categories are covered, arranged alphabetically for ease of use.

This book is not intended to replace regular, personal Bible study. Nor is it a replacement for a good concordance for in-depth study of a particular subject. It is, however, a quick reference to some of the key issues of life that women most often face.

We hope it will be an encouragement to you as you read.

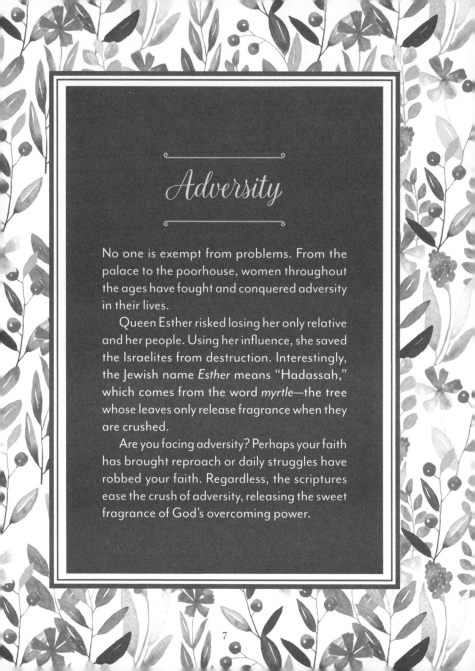

Adversity

No one is exempt from problems. From the palace to the poorhouse, women throughout the ages have fought and conquered adversity in their lives.

Queen Esther risked losing her only relative and her people. Using her influence, she saved the Israelites from destruction. Interestingly, the Jewish name *Esther* means "Hadassah," which comes from the word *myrtle*—the tree whose leaves only release fragrance when they are crushed.

Are you facing adversity? Perhaps your faith has brought reproach or daily struggles have robbed your faith. Regardless, the scriptures ease the crush of adversity, releasing the sweet fragrance of God's overcoming power.

I am sure that our suffering now cannot be compared
to the shining-greatness that He is going to give us.
ROMANS 8:18

As we have suffered much for Christ and have shared in
His pain, we also share His great comfort. But if we are in
trouble, it is for your good. And it is so you will be saved
from the punishment of sin. If God comforts us, it is for
your good also. You too will be given strength not to give
up when you have the same kind of trouble we have.
2 CORINTHIANS 1:5–6

If men speak bad of you because you are a
Christian, you will be happy because the Spirit
of shining-greatness and of God is in you.
1 PETER 4:14

"I have told you these things so you may have peace
in Me. In the world you will have much trouble.
But take hope! I have power over the world!"
JOHN 16:33

These tests have come to prove your faith and to show that it
is good. Gold, which can be destroyed, is tested by fire. Your
faith is worth much more than gold and it must be tested
also. Then your faith will bring thanks and shining-greatness and honor to Jesus Christ when He comes again.
1 PETER 1:7

I want to know Him. I want to have the same power in my
life that raised Jesus from the dead. I want to understand
and have a share in His sufferings and be like Christ in His
death. Then I may be raised up from among the dead.
PHILIPPIANS 3:10–11

After you have suffered for awhile, God Himself will make you perfect. He will keep you in the right way. He will give you strength. He is the God of all loving-favor and has called you through Christ Jesus to share His shining-greatness forever.
1 PETER 5:10

"You are happy when men hate you and do not want you around and put shame on you because you trust in Me."
LUKE 6:22

Is anyone among you suffering? He should pray.
JAMES 5:13

All who want to live a God-like life who belong to Christ Jesus will suffer from others.
2 TIMOTHY 3:12

The little troubles we suffer now for a short time are making us ready for the great things God is going to give us forever.
2 CORINTHIANS 4:17

If we suffer and stay true to Him, then we will be a leader with Him. If we say we do not know Him, He will say He does not know us.
2 TIMOTHY 2:12

• •

Our Creator never intended that we should shoulder a load of suffering ourselves. That's the whole purpose of spiritual community.
LINDA BARTLETT

Angels

A near miss. Your car swerves to the side of the road avoiding a collision with an oncoming vehicle. How did you avoid disaster?

Fatigue zaps your strength but you still have much to do. You pray and amazingly you breeze through your work as if unseen hands carried you to complete the task. A coincidence? Or did God dispatch angels to assist you?

Angels are real. Unlike the stereotypical images of chubby-cheeked cherubs, these powerful, angelic beings minister to believers. At God's command, they delivered Paul from prison, shut the lions' mouths, provided for Elijah, and brought an amazing message to Mary.

Chubby-cheeked cherubs? Think again.

God never said to any angel, "Sit at My right side, until I make those who hate You a place to rest Your feet." Are not all the angels spirits who work for God? They are sent out to help those who are to be saved from the punishment of sin.

HEBREWS 1:13–14

"He will send His angels with the loud sound of a horn. They will gather God's people together from the four winds. They will come from one end of the heavens to the other."

MATTHEW 24:31

The angel of the Lord stays close around those who fear Him, and He takes them out of trouble.

PSALM 34:7

For I know that nothing can keep us from the love of God. Death cannot! Life cannot! Angels cannot! Leaders cannot! Any other power cannot! Hard things now or in the future cannot! The world above or the world below cannot! Any other living thing cannot keep us away from the love of God which is ours through Christ Jesus our Lord.

ROMANS 8:38–39

• •

On life's busy thoroughfares we
meet with angels unawares. . . .
HELEN STEINER RICE

Anger

It doesn't matter who was right or wrong. You *feel* wronged and anger simmers on the verge of full boil.

Can we be angry and not sin? To feel anger is one thing, to act on it is another. When we use our anger to justify our wrongful deeds, we sin.

The Bible, however, gives us clear and concise instructions on how to handle anger or angry people. How can we curb anger, irritations, and flare-ups? Apply the calming influence of God's Word to our circumstance.

Ah, yes. That's better.

He who is slow to get angry has great understanding, but he who has a quick temper makes his foolish way look right.
PROVERBS 14:29

My Christian brothers, you know everyone should listen much and speak little. He should be slow to become angry. A man's anger does not allow him to be right with God.
JAMES 1:19–20

Do not have anything to do with a man given to anger or go with a man who has a bad temper. Or you might learn his ways and get yourself into a trap.
PROVERBS 22:24–25

Do not be quick in spirit to be angry. For anger is in the heart of fools.
ECCLESIASTES 7:9

It is better to live in a desert land than with a woman who argues and causes trouble.
PROVERBS 21:19

Fathers, do not be so hard on your children that they will give up trying to do what is right.
COLOSSIANS 3:21

A gentle answer turns away anger, but a sharp word causes anger.
PROVERBS 15:1

Be glad you can do the things you should be doing. Do all things without arguing and talking about how you wish you did not have to do them.
PHILIPPIANS 2:14

"But I tell you that whoever is angry with his brother will be guilty and have to suffer for his wrong-doing. Whoever says to his brother, 'You have no brains,' will have to stand in front of the court. Who-ever says, 'You fool,' will be sent to the fire of hell."
MATTHEW 5:22

A man with a bad temper starts fights, but he who is slow to anger quiets fighting.
PROVERBS 15:18

He who is slow to anger is better than the powerful. And he who rules his spirit is better than he who takes a city.
PROVERBS 16:32

Christian brothers, never pay back someone for the bad he has done to you. Let the anger of God take care of the other person. The Holy Writings say, "I will pay back to them what they should get, says the Lord."
ROMANS 12:19

A dry piece of food with peace and quiet is better than a house full of food with fighting.
PROVERBS 17:1

If you are angry, do not let it become sin. Get over your anger before the day is finished.
EPHESIANS 4:26

· ·

Being angry or unforgiving makes it impossible to have a gentle and quiet spirit.
DARLENE WILKINSON

Charity

Women are caregivers by nature. Need a hand? We offer two! Yet sometimes our gift of giving wears old under constant demands and daily responsibilities.

God, however, is the supreme example of charity at work. He saw our neediness and sent His Son, Jesus, to save us from our sins. And He keeps on giving.

Having received so much constrains us to give more liberally. God's charity never ceases, and neither should ours. Although needs differ—financial, physical, emotional, or spiritual—human benevolence comes from a giving heart. And our charitable giving begins right where we are.

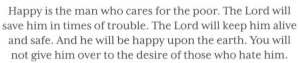

Happy is the man who cares for the poor. The Lord will save him in times of trouble. The Lord will keep him alive and safe. And he will be happy upon the earth. You will not give him over to the desire of those who hate him.
PSALM 41:1–2

He who shows kindness to a poor man gives to the Lord and He will pay him in return for his good act.
PROVERBS 19:17

"When you have a supper, ask poor people. Ask those who cannot walk and those who are blind. You will be happy if you do this. They cannot pay you back. You will get your pay when the people who are right with God are raised from the dead."
LUKE 14:13–14

He who hates his neighbor sins, but happy is he who shows loving-favor to the poor.
PROVERBS 14:21

"In every way I showed you that by working hard like this we can help those who are weak. We must remember what the Lord Jesus said, 'We are more happy when we give than when we receive.' "
ACTS 20:35

He has given much to the poor. His right-standing with God lasts forever. His horn will be lifted high in honor.
PSALM 112:9

I have been young, and now I am old. Yet I have never seen the man who is right with God left alone, or his children begging for bread. All day long he is kind and lets others use what he has. And his children make him happy.
PSALM 37:25–26

Tell those who are rich in this world not to be proud and not to trust in their money. Money cannot be trusted. They should put their trust in God. He gives us all we need for our happiness. Tell them to do good and be rich in good works. They should give much to those in need and be ready to share. Then they will be gathering together riches for themselves. These good things are what they will build on for the future. Then they will have the only true life!

1 TIMOTHY 6:17–19

"Sell what you have and give the money to poor people. Have money-bags for yourselves that will never wear out. These money-bags are riches in heaven that will always be there. No robber can take them and no bugs can eat them there. Your heart will be wherever your riches are."

LUKE 12:33–34

Most of all, have a true love for each other. Love covers many sins. Be happy to have people stay for the night and eat with you. God has given each of you a gift. Use it to help each other. This will show God's loving-favor.

1 PETER 4:8–10

"Give, and it will be given to you. You will have more than enough. It can be pushed down and shaken together and it will still run over as it is given to you. The way you give to others is the way you will receive in return."

LUKE 6:38

• •

Charity begins at home.
PROVERB

Comfort

A loved one passes away, and friends and family surround you with prayers and comforting words. Illness strikes a blow, but friends support and comfort you. Problems weigh heavy and there seems no way out, but the scriptures speak comfort to your heart.

Moms comfort their sick children with hugs and chicken soup. Similarly, God eases our pain and lightens our load through the comfort of His Word and His Spirit. Jesus called the Holy Spirit "the Comforter." He is the One who teaches, guides, soothes, and stands with us. The Comforter comforts like no one else can.

We give thanks to the God and Father of our Lord Jesus Christ.
He is our Father Who shows us loving-kindness and our God
Who gives us comfort. He gives us comfort in all our troubles. Then we can comfort other people who have the same
troubles. We give the same kind of comfort God gives us.

2 CORINTHIANS 1:3–4

Yes, even if I walk through the valley of the shadow of
death, I will not be afraid of anything, because You are
with me. You have a walking stick with which to guide
and one with which to help. These comfort me.

PSALM 23:4

"God will take away all their tears. There will
be no more death or sorrow or crying or pain.
All the old things have passed away."

REVELATION 21:4

"Then I will ask My Father and He will give you
another Helper. He will be with you forever."

JOHN 14:16

"But as for me, I would look to God.
I would put my troubles before God."

JOB 5:8

For the Lord Himself will come down from heaven with
a loud call. The head angel will speak with a loud voice.
God's horn will give its sounds. First, those who belong
to Christ will come out of their graves to meet the Lord.
Then, those of us who are still living here on earth will be
gathered together with them in the clouds. We will meet
the Lord in the sky and be with Him forever. Because
of this, comfort each other with these words.

1 THESSALONIANS 4:16–18

He will take away death for all time. The Lord God will dry tears from all faces. He will take away the shame of His people from all the earth. For the Lord has spoken.
ISAIAH 25:8

"Teach them to do all the things I have told you. And I am with you always, even to the end of the world."
MATTHEW 28:20

Add to my greatness, and turn to comfort me.
PSALM 71:21

"I will not leave you without help as children without parents. I will come to you."
JOHN 14:18

"Come to Me, all of you who work and have heavy loads. I will give you rest."
MATTHEW 11:28

I have remembered Your Law from a long time ago, O Lord, and I am comforted.
PSALM 119:52

"I will comfort you as one is comforted by his mother. And you will be comforted in Jerusalem."
ISAIAH 66:13

Last of all, Christian brothers, good-bye. Do that which makes you complete. Be comforted. Work to get along with others. Live in peace. The God of love and peace will be with you.
2 CORINTHIANS 13:11

Come close to God and He will come close to you. Wash your hands, you sinners. Clean up your hearts, you who want to follow the sinful ways of the world and God at the same time.
JAMES 4:8

The Spirit of the Lord God is on me, because the Lord has chosen me to bring good news to poor people. He has sent me to heal those with a sad heart. He has sent me to tell those who are being held and those in prison that they can go free. He has sent me to tell about the year of the Lord's favor, and the day our God will bring punishment. He has sent me to comfort all who are filled with sorrow.
ISAIAH 61:1–2

We give thanks to the God and Father of our Lord Jesus Christ. He is our Father Who shows us loving-kindness and our God Who gives us comfort. He gives us comfort in all our troubles. Then we can comfort other people who have the same troubles. We give the same kind of comfort God gives us. As we have suffered much for Christ and have shared in His pain, we also share His great comfort.
2 CORINTHIANS 1:3–5

• •

All you really need is the One who promised
never to leave or forsake you—the One
who said, "Lo, I am with you always."
JONI EARECKSON TADA

Conversation

Have you ever blurted out the wrong words at the wrong time? Mortified, you wish you could push rewind and start again—but unfortunately, the words are irretrievable.

The scriptures tell us to keep watch over our tongue, and for good reason. Words have the power to create strife or peace; to uplift or destroy; to bless or to curse.

The old adage claims "words will never hurt me." That, however, is untrue. Wrong words *do* hurt, but the right words spoken at the right time have the power to heal and comfort. Words count—so count your words!

The tongue is also a small part of the body, but it can speak big things. See how a very small fire can set many trees on fire.
JAMES 3:5

A word spoken at the right time is like fruit of gold set in silver.
PROVERBS 25:11

Do not hurry to speak or be in a hurry as you think what to tell God. For God is in heaven and you are on the earth. So let your words be few.
ECCLESIASTES 5:2

A gentle answer turns away anger, but a sharp word causes anger.
PROVERBS 15:1

The mind of the one who is right with God thinks about how to answer, but the mouth of the sinful pours out sinful things.
PROVERBS 15:28

Speak with them in such a way they will want to listen to you. Do not let your talk sound foolish. Know how to give the right answer to anyone.
COLOSSIANS 4:6

The heart of the wise has power over his mouth and adds learning to his lips. Pleasing words are like honey. They are sweet to the soul and healing to the bones.
PROVERBS 16:23–24

He who is always telling stories makes secrets known, but he who can be trusted keeps a thing hidden.
PROVERBS 11:13

He who is right in his walk is sure in his steps, but
he who takes the wrong way will be found out.
PROVERBS 10:9

Even if I talk about myself, I would not be a fool because it
is the truth. But I will say no more because I want no one to
think better of me than he does when he sees or hears me.
2 CORINTHIANS 12:6

A fool always loses his temper, but a wise man keeps quiet.
PROVERBS 29:11

Put out of your life these things also: anger, bad
temper, bad feelings toward others, talk that hurts
people, speaking against God, and dirty talk.
COLOSSIANS 3:8

O Lord, put a watch over my mouth.
Keep watch over the door of my lips.
PSALM 141:3

There is one whose foolish words cut like a sword,
but the tongue of the wise brings healing.
PROVERBS 12:18

We all make many mistakes. If anyone does not
make a mistake with his tongue by saying the wrong
things, he is a perfect man. It shows he is able to
make his body do what he wants it to do.
JAMES 3:2

· ·

Kind words can be short and easy to speak,
but their echoes are truly endless.
MOTHER TERESA

Counsel

Were you ever so immersed in a problem that you felt like you were drowning? Have you ever had to make a decision and didn't know what to do? At those times we turn to God—often through godly counsel, perhaps from a pastor or trusted Christian friend.

We all need counsel and direction sometimes. The old saying that "two heads are better than one" is not only noteworthy, it's scriptural!

King Solomon said that to seek godly counsel is wise. Moreover, to grow spiritually we must maintain an open, teachable spirit. Good advice comes from God-advice. Now that's good counsel.

God has given each of you a gift. Use it to help each other. This will show God's loving-favor.
1 PETER 4:10

For to us a Child will be born. To us a Son will be given. And the rule of the nations will be on His shoulders. His name will be called Wonderful, Teacher, Powerful God, Father Who Lives Forever, Prince of Peace.
ISAIAH 9:6

"All your sons will be taught by the Lord, and the well-being of your children will be great."
ISAIAH 54:13

There is no joy while we are being punished. It is hard to take, but later we can see that good came from it. And it gives us the peace of being right with God.
HEBREWS 12:11

Listen to words about what you should do, and take your punishment if you need it, so that you may be wise the rest of your days.
PROVERBS 19:20

"The Holy Spirit is coming. He will lead you into all truth. He will not speak His Own words. He will speak what He hears. He will tell you of things to come."
JOHN 16:13

A nation falls where there is no wise leading, but it is safe where there are many wise men who know what to do.
PROVERBS 11:14

Plans go wrong without talking together, but they will
go well when many wise men talk about what to do.
PROVERBS 15:22

"The Lord punishes everyone He loves. He whips every son He
receives." Do not give up when you are punished by God. Be
willing to take it, knowing that God is teaching you as a son.
Is there a father who does not punish his son sometimes?
HEBREWS 12:6–7

A wise man will hear and grow in learning.
A man of understanding will become able.
PROVERBS 1:5

Two are better than one, because they have good
pay for their work. For if one of them falls, the
other can help him up. But it is hard for the one
who falls when there is no one to lift him up.
ECCLESIASTES 4:9–10

. . . .

The true secret of giving advice is, after you have honestly
given it, to be perfectly indifferent whether it is taken or not,
and never persist in trying to set people right.
HANNAH WHITALL SMITH

Courage

Few of us require the kind of courage that Daniel had when he entered the lions' den or that David exercised when he confronted the giant. Nevertheless, courage is needed to conquer our fears, proclaim our faith, and overcome adversity. Oftentimes, we need courage just to get through the day!

The following verses provide instructions and admonitions to build our faith and fortitude. They equip us with the courage we need to conquer our giants in life's den of lions.

Wait for the Lord. Be strong. Let your heart
be strong. Yes, wait for the Lord.
PSALM 27:14

For God did not give us a spirit of fear. He gave us a
spirit of power and of love and of a good mind.
2 TIMOTHY 1:7

So we can say for sure, "The Lord is my Helper.
I am not afraid of anything man can do to me."
HEBREWS 13:6

And now, my children, live by the help of Him. Then when He
comes again, we will be glad to see Him and not be ashamed.
1 JOHN 2:28

The sinful run away when no one is trying to
catch them, but those who are right with God
have as much strength of heart as a lion.
PROVERBS 28:1

Be strong. Be strong in heart, all you who hope in the Lord.
PSALM 31:24

We can come to God without fear because
we have put our trust in Christ.
EPHESIANS 3:12

• •

You have to accept whatever comes and the
only important thing is that you meet it with
courage, and with the best you have to give.
ELEANOR ROOSEVELT

Diligence

The author of Ecclesiastes 9:10 wrote: "Whatever your hand finds to do, do it with all your strength." Diligence keeps going while frustration gives up. Diligence acts while procrastination rests. Diligence says, "I can do it" while defeat says, "I can't."

To work with diligence is essential to every facet of our spiritual and physical lives. With devoted tenacity we seek God and His will. With steadfast determination, we pray and study His Word.

Wherever we are or whatever we do, God calls us to remain diligent—even when our greatest efforts seem vain or our hard work goes unnoticed.

I remember my song in the night. I think with
my heart. And my spirit asks questions.
PSALM 77:6

"Only be very careful to obey the Law which the Lord's
servant Moses told you. Love the Lord your God. Walk
in all His ways. Obey His Laws. Stay close to Him,
and work for Him with all your heart and soul."
JOSHUA 22:5

The soul of the lazy person has strong desires
but gets nothing, but the soul of the one who
does his best gets more than he needs.
PROVERBS 13:4

He who works with a lazy hand is poor, but the
hand of the hard worker brings riches.
PROVERBS 10:4

But you, Christian brothers, do not get tired of doing good.
2 THESSALONIANS 3:13

If someone has the gift of speaking words of comfort and
help, he should speak. If someone has the gift of sharing what he has, he should give from a willing heart. If
someone has the gift of leading other people, he should
lead them. If someone has the gift of showing kindness to others, he should be happy as he does it.
ROMANS 12:8

Keep your heart pure for out of it are
he important things of life.
PROVERBS 4:23

The plans of those who do their best lead only to having all
they need, but all who are in a hurry come only to want.
PROVERBS 21:5

Do not let yourselves get tired of doing good. If we do not give up, we will get what is coming to us at the right time.
GALATIANS 6:9

Dear friends, since you are waiting for these things to happen, do all you can to be found by Him in peace. Be clean and free from sin.
2 PETER 3:14

"Whatever is wanted by the God of heaven, let it be done in full for the house of the God of heaven. Or else He might be angry with the nation of the king and his sons."
EZRA 7:23

So then, Christian brothers, because of all this, be strong. Do not allow anyone to change your mind. Always do your work well for the Lord. You know that whatever you do for Him will not be wasted.
1 CORINTHIANS 15:58

Much food is in the plowed land of the poor, but it is taken away because of wrong-doing.
PROVERBS 13:23

Whatever your hand finds to do, do it with all your strength. For there is no work or planning or learning or wisdom in the place of the dead where you are going.
ECCLESIASTES 9:10

• •

When I stand before God at the end of my life, I would hope that I would not have a single bit of talent left, and could say, "I used everything you gave me."
ERMA BOMBECK

Discipline, Family

Discipline in a Christian home consists of more than issuing commands like, "No video games until you finish your homework!" or, "Stop goofing around before someone gets hurt!"

It's easy to shout directives, but administering loving discipline takes work, thought, and persistence. To establish rules and lovingly implement them is to build structure, providing children with a sense of security. Discipline teaches kids the consequences of sin and the importance of submitting to authority.

Just as God disciplines those He loves, we discipline our children out of love. And contrary to popular thinking, a disciplined child is a happy child.

He should be a good leader in his own home. His children
must obey and respect him. If a man cannot be a good
leader in his own home, how can he lead the church?
1 TIMOTHY 3:4–5

Do not keep from punishing the child if he needs it.
If you beat him with the stick, he will not die. Beat
him with the stick, and save his soul from hell.
PROVERBS 23:13–14

A foolish way is held in the heart of a child, but
the punishing stick will send it far from him.
PROVERBS 22:15

Fathers, do not be so hard on your children that
they will give up trying to do what is right.
COLOSSIANS 3:21

A young man makes himself known by his actions
and proves if his ways are pure and right.
PROVERBS 20:11

Fathers, do not be too hard on your children
so they will become angry. Teach them in their
growing years with Christian teaching.
EPHESIANS 6:4

Punish your son when he does wrong and he will give
you comfort. Yes, he will give joy to your soul.
PROVERBS 29:17

• •

I can't think of anything parents could do to children
more heartless than failing to discipline.
JANETTE OKE

Discipline, God's

Ouch! Did you ever feel like God dispensed a spiritual spanking? Just as we discipline our children, our heavenly Father disciplines us. Why? Because an undisciplined life brings bondage while a disciplined life liberates. Yes, discipline frees us.

The Lord has a good reason for everything He does, and everything He does comes from love. So rather than bemoaning the temporary pain, consider discipline's benefits: It teaches, guides, garners appreciation, gives life, establishes our spiritual "daughtership," and yields the peaceable fruit of righteousness within us.

Admit it. Discipline helps way more than it hurts!

O Lord, do not speak sharp words to me in Your
anger, or punish me when You are angry.
PSALM 6:1

"I speak strong words to those I love and I punish
them. Have a strong desire to please the Lord.
Be sorry for your sins and turn from them."
REVELATION 3:19

"See, happy is the man to whom God speaks strong words.
So do not hate the strong teaching of the All-powerful. He
punishes, but He gives comfort. He hurts, but His hands heal."
JOB 5:17–18

Do you remember what God said to you when He called you
His sons? "My son, listen when the Lord punishes you. Do not
give up when He tells you what you must do. The Lord punishes everyone He loves. He whips every son He receives." Do
not give up when you are punished by God. Be willing to take
it, knowing that God is teaching you as a son. Is there a father
who does not punish his son sometimes? If you are not punished as all sons are, it means that you are not a true son of
God. You are not a part of His family and He is not your Father.
HEBREWS 12:5–8

"So know in your heart that the Lord your God was
punishing you just as a man punishes his son."
DEUTERONOMY 8:5

The Lord has punished me but He
has not given me over to death.
PSALM 118:18

But if we would look into our own lives and see if we
are guilty, then God would not have to say we are guilty.
When we are guilty, we are punished by the Lord so we
will not be told we are guilty with the rest of the world.
1 CORINTHIANS 11:31–32

For the word is a lamp. The teaching is a light, and
strong words that punish are the way of life.
PROVERBS 6:23

Happy is the man who is punished until he gives up sin,
O Lord, and whom You teach from Your Law. You give him
rest from days of trouble, until a hole is dug for the sinful.
PSALM 94:12–13

The Lord punishes everyone He loves.
He whips every son He receives.
PROVERBS 3:12

There is no joy while we are being punished. It is hard
to take, but later we can see that good came from it.
And it gives us the peace of being right with God.
HEBREWS 12:11

• •

God has to punish His children from time to time
and it is the very demonstration of His love.
ELISABETH ELLIOT

Duty

What is a Christian woman's duty? The scriptures list a few: to revere, serve, and obey God and keep His commandments.

In the 1940s and '50s a married woman's "duty" was clearly defined—to love and respect her husband while caring for her home and children. Today society has changed. God's Word, however, remains the same.

Our duty to love and respect our husbands, and care for our homes and children comes from our desire to follow biblical precepts. When we obey God and keep His commands, we automatically gain a sense of servitude toward our family and others.

What's our duty? To love God and follow His will.

The last word, after all has been heard, is: Honor God and
obey His Laws. This is all that every person must do.
ECCLESIASTES 12:13

"If you think it is wrong to serve the Lord, choose today
whom you will serve. Choose the gods your fathers
worshiped on the other side of the river, or choose the
gods of the Amorites in whose land you are living. But
as for me and my family, we will serve the Lord."
JOSHUA 24:15

"Now then, if you will obey My voice and keep My
agreement, you will belong to Me from among
all nations. For all the earth is Mine."
EXODUS 19:5

"Keep His Laws which I am giving you today. Then it may go
well with you and your children after you. And you may live
long in the land the Lord your God is giving you for all time."
DEUTERONOMY 4:40

When the ways of a man are pleasing to the Lord, He
makes even those who hate him to be at peace with him.
PROVERBS 16:7

"And why do you call Me, 'Lord, Lord,'
but do not do what I say?"
LUKE 6:46

"But I show loving-kindness to thousands of
those who love Me and keep My Laws."
EXODUS 20:6

"Be careful to listen to all these words I am telling you. Then it will go well with you and your children after you forever. For you will be doing what is good and right in the eyes of the Lord your God."

DEUTERONOMY 12:28

"You will be hated by all people because of Me. But he who stays true to the end will be saved."

MATTHEW 10:22

"See, I have put in front of you today life and what is good, and death and what is bad. I tell you today to love the Lord your God. Walk in His ways. Keep all His Laws and all that He has decided. Then you will live and become many. And the Lord your God will bring good to you in the land you are going in to take."

DEUTERONOMY 30:15–16

. . . .

Laziness may appear attractive,
but work gives satisfaction.

ANNE FRANK

Encouragement

A little encouragement goes a long way. It's been a bad week. You lost your car keys, burned your favorite recipe, misplaced important papers, ran late for work, and forgot a parent-teacher conference. Plus, your devotional time seems to have disappeared with those keys.

Discouraged, you enter church on Sunday fully prepared to force a fake smile. Instead, you're encouraged. The Sunday school lesson and sermon are just for you and the fellowship is great. Instantly, your deflated optimism fades into the distant past and you are revitalized, ready to share the encouragement you received with someone else.

Help each other. Speak day after day to each other while it is still today so your heart will not become hard by being fooled by sin.
HEBREWS 3:13

In each city they helped the Christians to be strong and true to the faith. They told them, "We must suffer many hard things to get into the holy nation of God."
ACTS 14:22

He must hold to the words of truth which he was taught. He must be able to teach the truth and show those who are against the truth that they are wrong.
TITUS 1:9

Let us not stay away from church meetings. Some people are doing this all the time. Comfort each other as you see the day of His return coming near.
HEBREWS 10:25

I can do all things because Christ gives me the strength.
PHILIPPIANS 4:13

So then, Christian brothers, keep a strong hold on what we have taught you by what we have said and by what we have written. Our Lord Jesus Christ and God our Father loves us. Through His loving-favor He gives us comfort and hope that lasts forever. May He give your hearts comfort and strength to say and do every good thing.
2 THESSALONIANS 2:15–17

So comfort each other and make each other strong as you are already doing.
1 THESSALONIANS 5:11

But if we are in trouble, it is for your good. And it is so you will be saved from the punishment of sin. If God comforts us, it is for your good also. You too will be given strength not to give up when you have the same kind of trouble we have.

2 CORINTHIANS 1:6

Help each other in troubles and problems.
This is the kind of law Christ asks us to obey.

GALATIANS 6:2

Do not always be thinking about your own plans only.
Be happy to know what other people are doing.

PHILIPPIANS 2:4

All the Holy Writings are God-given and are made alive by Him. Man is helped when he is taught God's Word. It shows what is wrong. It changes the way of a man's life. It shows him how to be right with God.

2 TIMOTHY 3:16

"When they take you to the places of worship and to the courts and to the leaders of the country, do not be worried about what you should say or how to say it. The Holy Spirit will tell you what you should say at that time."

LUKE 12:11–12

• •

What men and women need is encouragement. . . .
Instead of always harping on a man's faults, tell him of his virtues. Try to pull him out of his rut of bad habits.

ELEANOR H. PORTER

Eternity

Earthly life is short but eternity is forever. With that in mind, we all need to stand ready to meet the Lord.

Heaven is an actual place, not some mystical golden-gated wisp of cumulus clouds topped with angels. The most majestic places, ideals, and valued treasures can't compare to what God has prepared for those who love Him. And the best part about heaven is the One who rules and reigns there.

Right now, Jesus prepares your eternal home. And one day all of life's problems and trials will vanish in the light of an eternity with Him.

"There are many rooms in My Father's house. If it were not so, I would have told you. I am going away to make a place for you. After I go and make a place for you, I will come back and take you with Me. Then you may be where I am."
JOHN 14:2–3

There is a crown which comes from being right with God. The Lord, the One Who will judge, will give it to me on that great day when He comes again. I will not be the only one to receive a crown. All those who love to think of His coming and are looking for Him will receive one also.
2 TIMOTHY 4:8

Then I saw a new heaven and a new earth. The first heaven and the first earth had passed away. There was no more sea. I saw the Holy City, the new Jerusalem. It was coming down out of heaven from God. It was made ready like a bride is made ready for her husband.
REVELATION 21:1–2

For sure, I am telling you a secret. We will not all die, but we will all be changed. In a very short time, no longer than it takes for the eye to close and open, the Christians who have died will be raised. It will happen when the last horn sounds. The dead will be raised never to die again. Then the rest of us who are alive will be changed. Our human bodies made from dust must be changed into a body that cannot be destroyed. Our human bodies that can die must be changed into bodies that will never die. When this that can be destroyed has been changed into that which cannot be destroyed, and when this that does die has been changed into that which cannot die, then it will happen as the Holy Writings said it would happen. They said, "Death has no more power over life."
1 CORINTHIANS 15:51–54

He said to them, "You will suffer as I will suffer. But the places at My right side and at My left side are not Mine to give. Whoever My Father says will have those places."
MATTHEW 20:23

"I give them life that lasts forever. They will never be punished. No one is able to take them out of My hand."
JOHN 10:28

"Anyone who loves his life will lose it. Anyone who hates his life in this world will keep it forever."
JOHN 12:25

We are looking for what God has promised, which are new heavens and a new earth.
Only what is right and good will be there.
2 PETER 3:13

If a man does things to please his sinful old self, his soul will be lost. If a man does things to please the Holy Spirit, he will have life that lasts forever.
GALATIANS 6:8

When the Head Shepherd comes again, you will get the crown of shining-greatness that will not come to an end.
1 PETER 5:4

"Many of those who sleep in the dust of the earth will wake up. Some will have life that lasts forever, but others will have shame and will suffer much forever."
DANIEL 12:2

Jesus said to her, "I am the One Who raises the dead and gives them life. Anyone who puts his trust in Me will live again, even if he dies. Anyone who lives and has put his trust in Me will never die. Do you believe this?"
JOHN 11:25–26

Because you are not sorry for your sins and will not turn from them, you will be punished even more on the day of God's anger. God will be right in saying you are guilty. He will give to every man what he should get for the things he has done. Those who keep on doing good and are looking for His greatness and honor will receive life that lasts forever.
ROMANS 2:5–7

"Do not work for food that does not last. Work for food that lasts forever. The Son of Man will give you that kind of food. God the Father has shown He will do this."
JOHN 6:27

There will be no night there. There will be no need for a light or for the sun. Because the Lord God will be their light. They will be leaders forever.
REVELATION 22:5

The Holy Spirit raised Jesus from the dead. If the same Holy Spirit lives in you, He will give life to your bodies in the same way.
ROMANS 8:11

"You do read the Holy Writings. You think you have life that lasts forever just because you read them. They do tell of Me."
JOHN 5:39

. . . .

Redeemed, how I love to proclaim it!
His child, and forever, I am.
FANNIE CROSBY

Faith

You may be unaware of it, but you exercise faith daily. By faith you fall asleep, confident of morning. You eat, expecting nourishment. You breathe in air you can't see. You drive your car, trusting it will take you to your destination.

Jesus said that faith as tiny as a mustard seed is enough to produce miraculous results. So why do we assume that only mountain-moving faith will do? The Word of God is a faith-builder. So read on and cause that mustard seed to flourish and grow.

You must have faith as you ask Him. You must
not doubt. Anyone who doubts is like a wave
which is pushed around by the sea.
JAMES 1:6

The Lord said, "If your faith was as a mustard seed,
you could say to this tree, 'Be pulled out of the ground
and planted in the sea,' and it would obey you."
LUKE 17:6

You have never seen Him but you love Him. You cannot
see Him now but you are putting your trust in Him and
you have joy so great that words cannot tell about it.
1 PETER 1:8

Jesus heard this. He said to the leader of the Jewish
place of worship, "Do not be afraid, just believe."
MARK 5:36

You are now children of God because you
have put your trust in Christ Jesus.
GALATIANS 3:26

He gave the right and the power to become children of God to those who received Him. He gave
this to those who put their trust in His name.
JOHN 1:12

I pray that Christ may live in your hearts by faith. I pray
that you will be rooted with love. I pray that you will be able
to understand how wide and how long and how high and
how deep His love is. I pray that you will know the love
of Christ. His love is so great that even though we can understand some of it, it is so big you will be filled with God Himself.
EPHESIANS 3:17–19

He said to the woman, "Your faith has saved you from the punishment of sin. Go in peace."
LUKE 7:50

Jesus said to him, "Why do you ask Me that? The one who has faith can do all things."
MARK 9:23

"The early preachers wrote, 'They will all be taught of God.' Everyone who listens to the Father and learns from Him comes to Me."
JOHN 6:45

In this way, you do not have faith in Christ because of the wisdom of men. You have faith in Christ because of the power of God.
1 CORINTHIANS 2:5

Watch and keep awake! Stand true to the Lord. Keep on acting like men and be strong.
1 CORINTHIANS 16:13

If you say with your mouth that Jesus is Lord, and believe in your heart that God raised Him from the dead, you will be saved from the punishment of sin.
ROMANS 10:9

Jesus said to him, "Thomas, because you have seen Me, you believe. Those are happy who have never seen Me and yet believe!"
JOHN 20:29

A man cannot please God unless he has faith. Anyone who comes to God must believe that He is. That one must also know that God gives what is promised to the one who keeps on looking for Him.
HEBREWS 11:6

Our life is lived by faith. We do not live
by what we see in front of us.
2 Corinthians 5:7

Jesus said to them, "This is the work of God, that
you put your trust in the One He has sent."
John 6:29

"See! I stand at the door and knock. If anyone
hears My voice and opens the door, I will come
in to him and we will eat together."
Revelation 3:20

And so let us come near to God with a true heart full
of faith. Our hearts must be made clean from guilty
feelings and our bodies washed with pure water.
Hebrews 10:22

Jesus said to her, "Did I not say that if you would believe,
you would see the shining-greatness of God?"
John 11:40

I have been put up on the cross to die with Christ. I no
longer live. Christ lives in me. The life I now live in this
body, I live by putting my trust in the Son of God. He
was the One Who loved me and gave Himself for me.
Galatians 2:20

. . . .

Faith sees the invisible, believes the
unbelievable, and receives the impossible.
CORRIE TEN BOOM

Faithfulness of God

It's a fact. Even the most dependable people fail us: our husbands, our parents, our friends. They don't mean to—they're only human just as we are. On the other hand, we can fully depend on God's faithfulness at all times.

What God says, He does. His promises are true. What He did for His people and the prophets of old, He does for us today. We can safely trust Him at His word whatever the circumstance. Always remember: God cannot lie, and His faithfulness endures forever.

It's a fact!

We know that God makes all things work together for the good of those who love Him and are chosen to be a part of His plan.
ROMANS 8:28

O Lord, the heavens will praise Your great works and how faithful You are in the meeting of the holy ones.
PSALM 89:5

A faithful man will have many good things, but he who hurries to be rich will be punished for it.
PROVERBS 28:20

This truth also gives hope of life that lasts forever. God promised this before the world began. He cannot lie.
TITUS 1:2

So the Lord God says, "See, I lay in Jerusalem a Stone of great worth to build upon, a tested Stone. Anyone who puts his trust in Him will not be afraid of what will happen."
ISAIAH 28:16

"For the Lord your God is a God of loving-pity. He will not leave you or destroy you or forget the agreement He promised to your fathers."
DEUTERONOMY 4:31

Let us hold on to the hope we say we have and not be changed. We can trust God that He will do what He promised.
HEBREWS 10:23

"Do not be afraid of what you will suffer. Listen! The devil will throw some of you into prison to test you. You will be in trouble for ten days. Be faithful even to death. Then I will give you the crown of life."
REVELATION 2:10

"God is not a man, that He should lie. He is not a son of man, that He should be sorry for what He has said. Has He said, and will He not do it? Has He spoken, and will He not keep His Word?"
NUMBERS 23:19

"Thanks be to the Lord. He has given rest to His people Israel. He has done all that He promised. Every word has come true of all His good promise, which He promised through His servant Moses."
1 KINGS 8:56

Love the Lord, all you who belong to Him! The Lord keeps the faithful safe. But He gives the proud their pay in full.
PSALM 31:23

"Know then that the Lord your God is God, the faithful God. He keeps His promise and shows His loving-kindness to those who love Him and keep His Laws, even to a thousand family groups in the future."
DEUTERONOMY 7:9

The Lord is not slow about keeping His promise as some people think. He is waiting for you. The Lord does not want any person to be punished forever. He wants all people to be sorry for their sins and turn from them.
2 PETER 3:9

. . . .

God's designs regarding you, and His methods of bringing about these designs, are infinitely wise.
MADAME GUYON

Fearing God

Fear God? Aren't we supposed to trust, not fear the Lord? Fear isn't of God, right?

In the following verses we discover the definition of "fearing" God, and it's not what some people might think. The word *fear* is derived from the Greek word *eulabeia*, signifying caution and reverence.

When a godly fear and love are combined, they constitute a heartfelt devotion toward God. To fear the Lord is to reverence, love, respect, and honor Him. There's nothing scary about that!

"Do not be afraid of them who kill the body. They are not able to kill the soul. But fear Him Who is able to destroy both soul and body in hell."
MATTHEW 10:28

"Also, you should choose from the people able men who fear God, men of truth who hate to get things by doing wrong. Have these men rule over the people, as leaders of thousands, of hundreds, of fifties and of tens."
EXODUS 18:21

The fear of the Lord is the beginning of much learning. Fools hate wisdom and teaching.
PROVERBS 1:7

He said with a loud voice, "Honor God with love and fear. The time has come for Him to judge all men. Worship Him Who made heaven and earth and the sea and the places where water comes out of the earth."
REVELATION 14:7

"If only they had such a heart in them that they would fear Me and live by all My Laws always! Then it would go well with them and with their children forever."
DEUTERONOMY 5:29

The angel of the Lord stays close around those who fear Him, and He takes them out of trouble.
PSALM 34:7

A wise man fears God and turns away from what is sinful, but a fool is full of pride and is not careful.
PROVERBS 14:16

"So men honor Him with fear. He has respect for any who are wise in heart."
JOB 37:24

Since we have these great promises, dear friends,
let us turn away from every sin of the body or of
the spirit. Let us honor God with love and fear
by giving ourselves to Him in every way.
2 CORINTHIANS 7:1

He will fill the desire of those who fear Him.
He will also hear their cry and will save them.
PSALM 145:19

The secret of the Lord is for those who fear Him.
And He will make them know His agreement.
PSALM 25:14

" 'Do you not fear Me?' says the Lord. 'Do you not shake
in fear before Me? For I have placed the sand to be on
one side of the sea, a lasting wall that it cannot cross.
Even if there are waves, they cannot pass. Even if they
make much noise, they cannot cross over it.' "
JEREMIAH 5:22

Serve the Lord with fear, and be full of joy as you shake in fear.
PSALM 2:11

Then those who feared the Lord spoke often to one another,
and the Lord listened to them. And the names of those
who worshiped the Lord and honored Him were written down before Him in a Book to be remembered.
MALACHI 3:16

• •

Reverence for the Lord is the beginning of wisdom.
ELISABETH ELLIOT

Forgiveness

How do we forgive someone who has wronged us or hurt someone we love? How can we forgive when we don't *feel* forgiveness?

Corrie ten Boom, survivor of a women's Nazi concentration camp, wrote: "Forgiveness is an act of the will, and the will can function regardless of the temperature of the heart."

For every Christian, forgiveness is a choice. In order to fully receive God's forgiveness we must willingly extend forgiveness to others.

Through an act of her will, Corrie forgave her persecutors and her sister's murderers. Jesus forgave humankind of even more. How can we do less?

You must be kind to each other. Think of the other person. Forgive other people just as God forgave you because of Christ's death on the cross.
EPHESIANS 4:32

Try to understand other people. Forgive each other. If you have something against someone, forgive him. That is the way the Lord forgave you.
COLOSSIANS 3:13

When someone does something bad to you, do not do the same thing to him. When someone talks about you, do not talk about him. Instead, pray that good will come to him. You were called to do this so you might receive good things from God.
1 PETER 3:9

"If you forgive people their sins, your Father in heaven will forgive your sins also. If you do not forgive people their sins, your Father will not forgive your sins."
MATTHEW 6:14–15

Then Peter came to Jesus and said, "Lord, how many times may my brother sin against me and I forgive him, up to seven times?" Jesus said to him, "I tell you, not seven times but seventy times seven!"
MATTHEW 18:21–22

"If My people who are called by My name put away their pride and pray, and look for My face, and turn from their sinful ways, then I will hear from heaven. I will forgive their sin, and will heal their land."
2 CHRONICLES 7:14

"Watch yourselves! If your brother sins, speak sharp words to him. If he is sorry and turns from his sin, forgive him. What if he sins against you seven times in one day? If he comes to you and says he is sorry and turns from his sin, forgive him."
LUKE 17:3–4

"Forgive us our sins, as we forgive those who sin against us. Do not let us be tempted."
LUKE 11:4

But I tell you, do not fight with the man who wants to fight. Whoever hits you on the right side of the face, turn so he can hit the other side also. If any person takes you to court to get your shirt, give him your coat also. Whoever makes you walk a short way, go with him twice as far.
MATTHEW 5:39–41

"Forgive us our sins as we forgive those who sin against us."
MATTHEW 6:12

"Do not say what is wrong in other people's lives. Then other people will not say what is wrong in your life. Do not say someone is guilty. Then other people will not say you are guilty. Forgive other people and other people will forgive you."
LUKE 6:37

• •

If the wounds of millions are to be healed, what other way is there except through forgiveness?
CATHERINE MARSHALL

Friendship

Society uses the term *friendship* loosely. Social networking websites like Facebook connect us with scores of "friends" simultaneously—yet many of them are only acquaintances, not true friends.

The following passages unveil the meaning of a true friend. She's someone who brings out the best in you, who loves and gives unselfishly. She listens and speaks the truth with kindness—and when others criticize you, she stands in your defense.

Friendship is never one-sided because to have a friend, we must be a friend. Think of your very best girlfriend. Does she reflect the attributes of a true friend? Do you?

Iron is made sharp with iron, and one
man is made sharp by a friend.
PROVERBS 27:17

Jesus said to them, "If one of you has a friend and goes to
him in the night and says, 'Friend, give me three loaves
of bread, for a friend of mine is on a trip and has stopped
at my house. I have no food to give him.' The man inside
the house will say, 'Do not trouble me. The door is shut.
My children and I are in bed. I cannot get up and give
you bread.' I say to you, he may not get up and give him
bread because he is a friend. Yet, if he keeps on asking,
he will get up and give him as much as he needs."
LUKE 11:5–8

A friend loves at all times. A brother is born to share troubles.
PROVERBS 17:17

A man who has friends must be a friend, but there
is a friend who stays nearer than a brother.
PROVERBS 18:24

"Kindness from a friend should be shown to
a man without hope, or he might turn away
from the fear of the All-powerful."
JOB 6:14

• •

My friends are my estate.
EMILY DICKINSON

62

Generosity

Each Thanksgiving, Phyllis opens her home to the widows and singles of her church. She spends hours in meal preparations and sets the table with her finest china and best linens. Becky spends eight hours each week babysitting for young moms in need of a break. And for years, Lori and Esther have visited a local nursing home, sharing small gifts and homemade cookies with the residents.

Displays of generosity are as varied and numerous as the human fingerprint. Giving of our time, money, or talents is generous because we are giving of ourselves.

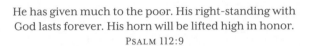

He has given much to the poor. His right-standing with
God lasts forever. His horn will be lifted high in honor.
PSALM 112:9

Do not keep good from those who should have it, when it is
in your power to do it. Do not say to your neighbor, "Go, and
return tomorrow, and I will give it," when you have it with you.
PROVERBS 3:27–28

He answered them, "If you have two coats, give one to him
who has none. If you have food, you must share some."
LUKE 3:11

"When you give to the poor, do not be as those who pretend to be someone they are not. They blow a horn in the
places of worship and in the streets so people may respect
them. For sure, I tell you, they have all the reward they are
going to get. When you give, do not let your left hand know
what your right hand gives. Your giving should be in secret.
Then your Father Who sees in secret will reward you."
MATTHEW 6:2–4

He who hates his neighbor sins, but happy is
he who shows loving-favor to the poor.
PROVERBS 14:21

"If your brother becomes poor and is not able to pay you
what he owes, then you should help him as you would
help a stranger or visitor. So he may live with you."
LEVITICUS 25:35

"The poor will always be in the land. So I
tell you to be free in giving to your brother,
to those in need, and to the poor in your land."
DEUTERONOMY 15:11

If you have any women whose husbands have died in your family, you must care for them. The church should not have to help them. The church can help women whose husbands have died who are all alone in this world and have no one else to help them.
1 TIMOTHY 5:16

He saw a poor woman whose husband had died. She put in two very small pieces of money. He said, "I tell you the truth, this poor woman has put in more than all of them. For they have put in a little of the money they had no need for. She is very poor and has put in all she had. She has put in what she needed for her own living."
LUKE 21:2–4

What if a Christian does not have clothes or food? ¹⁶ And one of you says to him, "Goodbye, keep yourself warm and eat well." But if you do not give him what he needs, how does that help him?
JAMES 2:15–16

Happy is the man who cares for the poor. The Lord will save him in times of trouble. The Lord will keep him alive and safe. And he will be happy upon the earth. You will not give him over to the desire of those who hate him.
PSALM 41:1–2

Each man should give as he has decided in his heart. He should not give, wishing he could keep it. Or he should not give if he feels he has to give. God loves a man who gives because he wants to give.
2 CORINTHIANS 9:7

He who shows kindness to a poor man gives to the Lord and He will pay him in return for his good act.
PROVERBS 19:17

"Is it not a time to share your food with the hungry, and bring the poor man into your house who has no home of his own? Is it not a time to give clothes to the person you see who has no clothes, and a time not to hide yourself from your own family? Then your light will break out like the early morning, and you will soon be healed. Your right and good works will go before you. And the shining-greatness of the Lord will keep watch behind you."

ISAIAH 58:7–8

"For sure, I tell you, whoever gives you a cup of water to drink in My name because you belong to Christ will not lose his reward from God."

MARK 9:41

"Give, and it will be given to you. You will have more than enough. It can be pushed down and shaken together and it will still run over as it is given to you. The way you give to others is the way you will receive in return."

LUKE 6:38

"In every way I showed you that by working hard like this we can help those who are weak. We must remember what the Lord Jesus said, 'We are more happy when we give than when we receive.' "

ACTS 20:35

• •

It's not how much we give but how much love we put into giving.

MOTHER TERESA

Gentleness

Dr. James Dobson, Christian psychologist and author, recalls the gentleness his wife exhibited whenever she awakened their then-small daughter from a nap. Standing nearby, Dobson would watch as Shirley gently stirred their child from slumber with her soft, sweet, soothing words. Her genteel manner impacted the renowned psychologist so much that he spoke of it many years later.

How we approach people matters. Are we brazen and critical? Or are we compassionate, seasoning our words with kindness? Gentleness is a fruit of the Spirit that brings much-needed relief in a harsh world.

"Follow My teachings and learn from Me. I am gentle and do not have pride. You will have rest for your souls."
MATTHEW 11:29

But those who have no pride will be given the earth. And they will be happy and have much more than they need.
PSALM 37:11

I, Paul, ask you this myself. I do it through Christ Who is so gentle and kind. Some people say that I am gentle and quiet when I am with you, but that I have no fear and that my language is strong when I am away from you.
2 CORINTHIANS 10:1

Teach your people to obey the leaders of their country. They should be ready to do any good work. They must not speak bad of anyone, and they must not argue. They should be gentle and kind to all people.
TITUS 3:1–2

He will feed His flock like a shepherd. He will gather the lambs in His arms and carry them close to His heart. He will be gentle in leading those that are with young.
ISAIAH 40:11

But the fruit that comes from having the Holy Spirit in our lives is: love, joy, peace, not giving up, being kind, being good, having faith.
GALATIANS 5:22

He leads those without pride into what is
right, and teaches them His way.
PSALM 25:9

For the Lord is happy with His people. He saves those
who have no pride and makes them beautiful.
PSALM 149:4

But the wisdom that comes from heaven is first of all
pure. Then it gives peace. It is gentle and willing to obey.
It is full of loving-kindness and of doing good. It has no
doubts and does not pretend to be something it is not.
JAMES 3:17

The Lord lifts up those who are suffering, and
He brings the sinful down to the ground.
PSALM 147:6

"You have given me the covering of Your saving
power. Your help makes me strong."
2 SAMUEL 22:36

Instead, we were gentle when we came to you.
We were like a mother caring for her children.
1 THESSALONIANS 2:7

• •

Take my heart and make it your dwelling place so
that everyone I touch will be touched also by you!
ALICE JOYCE DAVIDSON

God's Love

Have you ever read 1 Corinthians 13—the "Love Chapter"? The Living Bible says that love is patient and kind; never boastful, selfish, or rude. Love never demands its own way or is glad about injustice—rather, love rejoices when the truth wins out. Love is loyal no matter the cost. Love always believes the best in us and stands its ground in defending us.

Now substitute the word *love* with "God" and read that paragraph again. You see, God not only loves—He *is* love. No other love in heaven or on earth compares to God's because His very nature defines *agape*—selfless, unconditional—love. And that's how God loves us.

See what great love the Father has for us that He
would call us His children. And that is what we are.
For this reason the people of the world do not know
who we are because they did not know Him.
1 JOHN 3:1

God has shown His love to us by sending His only Son into the
world. God did this so we might have life through Christ.
1 JOHN 4:9

"I will bring My people back to Me. I will not hold back My
love from them, for I am no longer angry with them."
HOSEA 14:4

The Holy Writings say, "No eye has ever seen or no ear has
ever heard or no mind has ever thought of the wonderful things God has made ready for those who love Him."
1 CORINTHIANS 2:9

For I know that nothing can keep us from the love of God.
Death cannot! Life cannot! Angels cannot! Leaders cannot!
Any other power cannot! Hard things now or in the future
cannot! The world above or the world below cannot! Any
other living thing cannot keep us away from the love of
God which is ours through Christ Jesus our Lord.
ROMANS 8:38–39

Hope never makes us ashamed because the
love of God has come into our hearts through
the Holy Spirit Who was given to us.
ROMANS 5:5

The Lord takes care of all who love Him.
But He will destroy all the sinful.
PSALM 145:20

"For God so loved the world that He gave His only Son. Whoever puts his trust in God's Son will not be lost but will have life that lasts forever."
JOHN 3:16

But God showed His love to us. While we were still sinners, Christ died for us.
ROMANS 5:8

Because the Father loves you. He loves you because you love Me and believe that I came from the Father.
JOHN 16:27

• •

Love has its source in God, for love is the very essence of His being.
KAY ARTHUR

God's Provision

In recent years, a failing economy has caused much distress. People have lost their jobs and homes, and parents wonder how they will support their families. Yet it doesn't take a job loss to experience a financial drain, resulting in a shortage of basic necessities.

The following scriptures encourage us with words of hope and promise. Every Christian has the assurance of God's provision during tough times. As we wisely manage our money and trust in His promises, the Lord supplies— perhaps not our wants—but every one of our needs.

The young lions suffer want and hunger. But they who
look for the Lord will not be without any good thing.
PSALM 34:10

He gives food to those who fear Him. He will
remember His agreement forever.
PSALM 111:5

And my God will give you everything you need
because of His great riches in Christ Jesus.
PHILIPPIANS 4:19

Tell those who are rich in this world not to be proud
and not to trust in their money. Money cannot
be trusted. They should put their trust in God.
He gives us all we need for our happiness.
1 TIMOTHY 6:17

I have been young, and now I am old. Yet I have
never seen the man who is right with God left
alone, or his children begging for bread.
PSALM 37:25

• •

Lift up your eyes. Your heavenly Father waits to
bless you in inconceivable ways to make your
life what you never dreamed it could be.
ANNE ORTLUND

Gratitude

Evangelist Joyce Meyer has said, "Christians need an attitude of gratitude!"

Though we know that God frowns on murmuring and complaining, we do it anyway. We grumble about long stoplights, difficult neighbors, the weather, our jobs, family members, or household chores. Instead of thanking God for our blessings, we approach life with resignation rather than anticipation and gratefulness.

But what if we adjusted our attitude? We might just be happy! God's Word motivates us to discover and maintain a thankful spirit. Try it! Seize an attitude of gratitude.

Then He took the cup and gave thanks. He gave it
to them and said, "You must all drink from it."
MATTHEW 26:27

I will speak with the voice of thanks, and
tell of all Your great works.
PSALM 26:7

"Thanks be to the Lord. He has given rest to His
people Israel. He has done all that He promised.
Every word has come true of all His good promise,
which He promised through His servant Moses."
1 KINGS 8:56

O Lord, You have brought me up from the grave. You have
kept me alive, so that I will not go down into the deep.
PSALM 30:3

The man who worships on a special day does it to
honor the Lord. The man who eats meat does it to
honor the Lord. He gives thanks to God for what he
eats. The other man does not eat meat. In this way,
he honors the Lord. He gives thanks to God also.
ROMANS 14:6

O Lord my God, many are the great works You
have done, and Your thoughts toward us. No one
can compare with You! If I were to speak and tell
of them, there would be too many to number.
PSALM 40:5

I will give thanks to the Lord with all my heart. I will tell of all the great things You have done. I will be glad and full of joy because of You. I will sing praise to Your name, O Most High.
PSALM 9:1–2

Honor and thanks be to the Lord, Who carries our heavy loads day by day. He is the God Who saves us.
PSALM 68:19

In everything give thanks. This is what God wants you to do because of Christ Jesus.
1 THESSALONIANS 5:18

Give thanks to the Lord, for He is good, for His loving-kindness lasts forever.
PSALM 136:1

Then He took the seven loaves of bread and the fish and gave thanks. He broke them and gave them to His followers. The followers gave them to the people.
MATTHEW 15:36

It is good to give thanks to the Lord, and sing praises to Your name, O Most High. It is good to tell of Your loving-kindness in the morning, and of how faithful You are at night,
PSALM 92:1–2

• •

Simple gratitude helps us experience God at work in every moment of every day.
HARRIET CROSBY

Honesty

The cashier gives you too much money in change. Do you tell her? Out-of-town friends call unexpectedly and ask to stop by. Your house is a mess, you're dead tired, and you're in your pajamas. What do you say?

These scenarios happen all the time, giving us an opportunity to shine with honesty or dim with deceit. God's Word tells us to be aboveboard and upright in our dealings with others.

The old adage says, "Honesty is the best policy." Yet it's more than that. Honesty is a way of life.

Christian brothers, keep your minds thinking about whatever is true, whatever is respected, whatever is right, whatever is pure, whatever can be loved, and whatever is well thought of. If there is anything good and worth giving thanks for, think about these things.
PHILIPPIANS 4:8

You who are servants who are owned by someone, obey your owners. Work hard for them all the time, not just when they are watching you. Work for them as you would for the Lord because you honor God.
COLOSSIANS 3:22

"Do not steal. Be honest in what you do. Do not lie to one another."
LEVITICUS 19:11

Night is almost gone. Day is almost here. We must stop doing the sinful things that are done in the dark. We must put on all the things God gives us to fight with for the day. We must act all the time as if it were day. Keep away from wild parties and do not be drunk. Keep yourself free from sex sins and bad actions. Do not fight or be jealous.
ROMANS 13:12–13

Pray for us. Our hearts tell us we are right. We want to do the right thing always.
HEBREWS 13:18

Do your best to live a quiet life. Learn to do your own work well. We told you about this before. By doing this, you will be respected by those who are not Christians. Then you will not be in need and others will not have to help you.
1 THESSALONIANS 4:11–12

Live in peace with each other. Do not act or think with pride. Be happy to be with poor people. Keep yourself from thinking you are so wise. When someone does something bad to you, do not pay him back with something bad. Try to do what all men know is right and good.
ROMANS 12:16–17

Do not lie to each other. You have put out of your life your old ways. You have now become a new person and are always learning more about Christ. You are being made more like Christ. He is the One Who made you.
COLOSSIANS 3:9–10

We want to do the right thing. We want God and men to know we are honest.
2 CORINTHIANS 8:21

He gives money to be used without being paid for its use. And he does not take money to hurt those who are not guilty. He who does these things will never be shaken.
PSALM 15:5

I always try to live so my own heart tells me I am not guilty before God or man.
ACTS 24:16

"You know the Laws, 'Do not be guilty of sex sins in marriage. Do not kill another person. Do not take things from people in wrong ways. Do not steal. Do not lie. Respect your father and mother.'"
MARK 10:19

He who has clean hands and a pure heart. He who has not lifted up his soul to what is not true, and has not made false promises.
PSALM 24:4

Receive us into your hearts. We have done no wrong to anyone. We have not led anyone in the wrong way. We have not used anyone for our good.

2 CORINTHIANS 7:2

He who walks with God, and whose words are good and honest, he who will not take money received from wrong-doing, and will not receive money given in secret for wrong-doing, he who stops his ears from hearing about killing, and shuts his eyes from looking at what is sinful, he will have a place on high. His safe place will be a rock that cannot be taken over. He will be given food and will have water for sure.

ISAIAH 33:15–16

Tax-gatherers came to be baptized also. They asked him, "Teacher, what are we to do?" 13 He said to them, "Do not take more money from people than you should."

LUKE 3:12–13

"I hold on to what is right and good and will not let it go. My heart does not put me to shame for any of my days."

JOB 27:6

. . . .

Do not do what you would undo if caught.

LEAH ARENDT

Honor

To honor is to highly esteem someone for their integrity, honesty, uprightness, or courage. We pay homage to our veterans for their service to our country; we laud athletes, students, entertainers, ministers, and others who achieve excellence in their fields. In other words, we honor people we value and deem worthy of our respect.

The below verses tell us to honor the Lord with our tithes, our adoration, and everything we have. Far above all others, God is worthy of *all* our honor and praise.

Honor the Lord with your riches,
and with the first of all you grow.
PROVERBS 3:9

Children, as Christians, obey your parents. This is the
right thing to do. Respect your father and mother. This
is the first Law given that had a promise. The promise is
this: If you respect your father and mother, you will live a
long time and your life will be full of many good things
EPHESIANS 6:1–3

She is worth more than stones of great worth. Nothing you can wish for compares with her. Long life is in
her right hand. Riches and honor are in her left hand.
PROVERBS 3:15–16

"Honor your father and your mother, so your life may
be long in the land the Lord your God gives you."
EXODUS 20:12

• •

Let our actions make us worthy of the blessing we have
received and [pray] that God will continue to bless us!
DIANE ALBERS

Hope

Have you ever hoped for something? Maybe a bigger house? A smaller dress size? A day to yourself? Or maybe more serious things like a physical healing or restoration of your marriage?

The word *hope* in the Greek translation is *elpis*, meaning "confident expectation in the unseen future" or "the happy expectation of good." Hope launches a positive outlook. Without it, lives remain fragmented and broken, personal dreams go unrealized, and sick hearts lose the capacity to cope.

Hope tells you to hold on in anticipation and expectation—because something good is just ahead!

" 'For I know the plans I have for you,' says
the Lord, 'plans for well-being and not for
trouble, to give you a future and a hope.'"
JEREMIAH 29:11

Dear friends, we are God's children now. But it has not
yet been shown to us what we are going to be. We know
that when He comes again, we will be like Him because we
will see Him as He is. The person who is looking for this to
happen will keep himself pure because Christ is pure
1 JOHN 3:2–3

We are glad for our troubles also. We know that troubles help us learn not to give up. ⁴When we have learned
not to give up, it shows we have stood the test. When we
have stood the test, it gives us hope. Hope never makes
us ashamed because the love of God has come into our
hearts through the Holy Spirit Who was given to us.
ROMANS 5:3–5

The hope of those who are right with God is joy,
but the hope of the sinful comes to nothing.
PROVERBS 10:28

Let us thank the God and Father of our Lord Jesus Christ.
It was through His loving-kindness that we were born
again to a new life and have a hope that never dies. This
hope is ours because Jesus was raised from the dead.
1 PETER 1:3

"Good will come to the man who trusts in the
Lord, and whose hope is in the Lord"
JEREMIAH 17:7

My soul becomes weak with desire for Your saving
power, but I have put my hope in Your Word.
PSALM 119:81

"The Lord is my share." says my soul, "so I have hope in Him." The Lord is good to those who wait for Him, to the one who looks for Him. It is good that one should be quiet and wait for the saving power of the Lord.
LAMENTATIONS 3:24–26

Because we are men of the day, let us keep our minds awake. Let us cover our chests with faith and love. Let us cover our heads with the hope of being saved.
1 THESSALONIANS 5:8

Your heart should be holy and set apart for the Lord God. Always be ready to tell everyone who asks you why you believe as you do. Be gentle as you speak and show respect.
1 PETER 3:15

This truth also gives hope of life that lasts forever. God promised this before the world began. He cannot lie.
TITUS 1:2

We are waiting for the hope of being made right with God. This will come through the Holy Spirit and by faith.
GALATIANS 5:5

But Christ was faithful as a Son Who is Head of God's house. We are of God's house if we keep our trust in the Lord until the end. This is our hope.
HEBREWS 3:6

Our hope comes from God. May He fill you with joy and peace because of your trust in Him. May your hope grow stronger by the power of the Holy Spirit.
ROMANS 15:13

I hope for Your saving power, O Lord, and I follow Your Word.
PSALM 119:166

God wants these great riches of the hidden truth to be made known to the people who are not Jews. The secret is this: Christ in you brings hope of all the great things to come.

COLOSSIANS 1:27

Because of Christ, you have put your trust in God. He raised Christ from the dead and gave Him great honor. So now your faith and hope are in God.

1 PETER 1:21

I trust God for the same things they are looking for. I am looking for the dead to rise, both those right with God and the sinful.

ACTS 24:15

We want each one of you to keep on working to the end. Then what you hope for, will happen.

HEBREWS 6:11

There is one body and one Spirit. There is one hope in which you were called.

EPHESIANS 4:4

We speak without fear because our trust is in Christ.

2 CORINTHIANS 3:12

I pray that your hearts will be able to understand. I pray that you will know about the hope given by God's call. I pray that you will see how great the things are that He has promised to those who belong to Him.

EPHESIANS 1:18

I hope very much that I will have no reason to be ashamed. I hope to honor Christ with my body if it be by my life or by my death. I want to honor Him without fear, now and always.

PHILIPPIANS 1:20

Remember Your Word to Your servant,
for You have given me hope.
PSALM 119:49

Why are you sad, O my soul? Why have you
become troubled within me? Hope in God, for I
will yet praise Him, my help and my God.
PSALM 42:11

We thank God for the hope that is being kept for you
in heaven. You first heard about this hope through
the Good News which is the Word of Truth.
COLOSSIANS 1:5

We are to be looking for the great hope and the coming
of our great God and the One Who saves, Christ Jesus.
TITUS 2:13

Now faith is being sure we will get what we hope
for. It is being sure of what we cannot see.
HEBREWS 11:1

But those in need will not always be forgotten.
The hope of the poor will not be lost forever.
PSALM 9:18

• •

Optimism is the faith that leads to achievement.
Nothing can be done without hope and confidence.
HELEN KELLER

Hospitality

Women and hospitality go together like coffee and cream. Generally, women are the ones who host family gatherings, church dinners, kids' birthday parties, and so much more.

Back in the 1930s and '40s, vagabonds would often go house to house for food. Without hesitation, the woman of the house would serve the stranger a hot meal. Of course, that kind of hospitality is danger to us today. Yet we should continue to open our homes and give to those we *do* know.

After all, a hospitable woman not only opens her home, she opens her heart.

Do not forget to be kind to strangers and let
them stay in your home. Some people have had
angels in their homes without knowing it.
HEBREWS 13:2

"If a stranger lives with you in your land, do not do
wrong to him. You should act toward the stranger
who lives among you as you would toward one born
among you. Love him as you love yourself. For you were
strangers in the land of Egypt. I am the Lord your God."
LEVITICUS 19:33–34

Wisdom has built her house. She has made seven pillars
to hold it up. She has cooked her food, and has mixed
her wine, and she has set her table. She has sent out the
young women who work for her. She calls from the highest
places of the city, "Whoever is easy to fool, let him turn in
here!" She says to the one without understanding, "Come
and eat my food, and drink the wine I have mixed."
PROVERBS 9:1–5

"When you have a supper, ask poor people. Ask those who
cannot walk and those who are blind. You will be happy if you
do this. They cannot pay you back. You will get your pay when
the people who are right with God are raised from the dead."
LUKE 14:13–14

She must be known for doing good things for people
and for being a good mother. She must be known for
taking strangers into her home and for washing the
feet of Christians. She must be known for helping
those who suffer and for showing kindness.
1 TIMOTHY 5:10

"Do not gather what is left among your vines, or gather the grapes that have fallen. Leave them for those in need and for the stranger. I am the Lord your God."
LEVITICUS 19:10

What if a Christian does not have clothes or food? And one of you says to him, "Goodbye, keep yourself warm and eat well." But if you do not give him what he needs, how does that help him?
JAMES 2:15–16

"He does what is right and fair for the child without parents and the woman whose husband has died. He shows His love for the stranger by giving him food and clothing."
DEUTERONOMY 10:18

Share what you have with Christian brothers who are in need. Give meals and a place to stay to those who need it.
ROMANS 12:13

Be happy to have people stay for the night and eat with you.
1 PETER 4:9

For sure, I tell you, whoever gives you a cup of water to drink in My name because you belong to Christ will not lose his reward from God.
MARK 9:41

• •

Just allow your guest to feel at ease because you are, whatever the state of your house. This is an important element to being a gracious host.
LINDA DAVIS ZUMBEHL

Humility

Nineteenth-century missionary Mary Slessor said: "Blessed is the man or woman who is able to serve cheerfully in the second rank—a big test."

Serving in the limelight is one thing, but serving absent of accolades and applause is another. Those who take a backseat and work as hard as if they were in the front seat are diligent. But those who take a backseat and have no thought of taking credit for their deeds are humble.

Jesus said, "The first shall be last and the last shall be first" in God's kingdom. Humility leads to greatness, and great people are the ones who are humble.

Live in peace with each other. Do not act or think
with pride. Be happy to be with poor people. Keep
yourself from thinking you are so wise.
ROMANS 12:16

The Lord says, "Let not a wise man speak with
pride about his wisdom. Let not the strong man
speak with pride about his strength. And let not a
rich man speak with pride about his riches.
JEREMIAH 9:23

If I must talk about myself, I will do it about
the things that show how weak I am.
2 CORINTHIANS 11:30

Do not talk much about tomorrow, for you
do not know what a day will bring.
PROVERBS 27:1

Whoever is without pride as this little child is
the greatest in the holy nation of heaven.
MATTHEW 18:4

"For God puts down the man who is filled with
pride. But He saves the one who is not proud."
JOB 22:29

O Lord, my heart is not proud. My eyes are not
filled with pride. And I do not trouble myself with
important things or in things too great for me.
PSALM 131:1

"Those who know there is nothing good in themselves
are happy, because the holy nation of heaven is theirs."
MATTHEW 5:3

In the same way, you younger men must obey the church leaders. Be gentle as you care for each other. God works against those who have pride. He gives His loving-favor to those who do not try to honor themselves. So put away all pride from yourselves. You are standing under the powerful hand of God. At the right time He will lift you up.
1 PETER 5:5–6

"Listen to me, you who are following what is right and good, and who are looking for the Lord. Look to the rock from which you were cut out, and to the hole from which you were dug."
ISAIAH 51:1

O Lord, You have heard the prayers of those
who have no pride. You will give strength to
their heart, and You will listen to them.
PSALM 10:17

God makes fun of those who make fun of the truth
but gives loving-favor to those who have no pride.
PROVERBS 3:34

"The person who thinks he is important will find out
how little he is worth. The person who is not trying
to honor himself will be made important."
MATTHEW 23:12

He put aside everything that belonged to Him and made Himself the same as a servant who is owned by someone. He became human by being born as a man. After He became a man, He gave up His important place and obeyed by dying on a cross. Because of this, God lifted Jesus high above everything else. He gave Him a name that is greater than any other name
PHILIPPIANS 2:7–9

When pride comes, then comes shame, but
wisdom is with those who have no pride.
PROVERBS 11:2

For even if the Lord is honored, He thinks about those who
have no pride. But He knows the proud from far away.
PSALM 138:6

For the high and honored One Who lives forever, Whose
name is Holy, says, "I live in the high and holy place.
And I also live with those who are sorry for their sins
and have turned from them and are not proud. I give
new strength to the spirit of those without pride, and
also to those whose hearts are sorry for their sins."
ISAIAH 57:15

For He Who punishes for the blood of another remembers
them. He does not forget the cry of those who suffer.
PSALM 9:12

Let yourself be brought low before the Lord.
Then He will lift you up and help you.
JAMES 4:10

· ·

All of the charm and beauty a woman may have
amounts to nothing if her ambitions are self-
centered. But if she reflects her Creator and assumes
the posture of a graceful servant, she cannot
help but command high respect and love.
JEANNE HENDRICKS

Joy

Do you know someone who has a spirit of joy? No matter what happens in life, she always has an uplifting word and a glowing smile. She sparkles with joy brighter than polished diamonds and, not surprisingly, everyone enjoys her company.

The scriptures encourage us to delight in the Lord that way—to illuminate with joy about our salvation and the goodness of God. Our joy should shine in such a way that it lights the pathway to lead others to Christ.

One day, we will rejoice in heaven. That fact alone should cause us to jump for joy!

The angel said to them, "Do not be afraid. See! I bring you good news of great joy which is for all people."
LUKE 2:10

The Lord is my strength and my safe cover. My heart trusts in Him, and I am helped. So my heart is full of joy. I will thank Him with my song.
PSALM 28:7

Be full of joy always because you belong to the Lord. Again I say, be full of joy!
PHILIPPIANS 4:4

"Until now you have not asked for anything in My name. Ask and you will receive. Then your joy will be full."
JOHN 16:24

Be glad in the Lord and be full of joy, you who are right with God! Sing for joy all you who are pure in heart!
PSALM 32:11

A sinful man is trapped by his sins, but a man who is right with God sings for joy.
PROVERBS 29:6

We are full of sorrow and yet we are always happy. We are poor and yet we make many people rich. We have nothing and yet we have everything.
2 CORINTHIANS 6:10

"His owner said to him, 'You have done well. You are a good and faithful servant. You have been faithful over a few things. I will put many things in your care. Come and share my joy.'"
MATTHEW 25:21

"Be glad in that day. Be full of joy for your reward is much in heaven. Their fathers did these things to the early preachers."
LUKE 6:23

Call out with joy to the Lord, all the earth. Be glad as you serve the Lord. Come before Him with songs of joy.
PSALM 100:1–2

"But now I come to You, Father. I say these things while I am in the world. In this way, My followers may have My joy in their hearts."
JOHN 17:13

All the days of the suffering are hard, but a glad heart has a special supper all the time.
PROVERBS 15:15

We are not the boss of your faith but we are working with you to make you happy. Your faith is strong.
2 CORINTHIANS 1:24

Is anyone among you suffering? He should pray. Is anyone happy? He should sing songs of thanks to God.
JAMES 5:13

Tell of your joy to each other by singing the Songs of David and church songs. Sing in your heart to the Lord.
EPHESIANS 5:19

I will have much joy in the Lord. My soul will have joy in my God, for He has clothed me with the clothes of His saving power. He has put around me a coat of what is right and good, as a man at his own wedding wears something special on his head, and as a bride makes herself beautiful with stones of great worth.
ISAIAH 61:10

• •

Laughter lightens the load.
PATSY CLAIRMONT

Kindness

Years ago, Oprah Winfrey encouraged her audience to engage in "random acts of kindness." She led the crusade through personal example with deeds such as paying the toll for the person in the vehicle behind her. Her message was simple: Extend one act of kindness to a stranger each day.

Kindness is rooted in a giving heart. The virtue is displayed in small ways like driving an elderly patient to the doctor, cooking a meal for a shut-in, babysitting for a busy mom, or simply sharing a smile.

When kindness is the rule, there's nothing random about it.

Give to any person who asks you for something. If a person
takes something from you, do not ask for it back.
LUKE 6:30

When someone does something bad to you, do not do the
same thing to him. When someone talks about you, do not talk
about him. Instead, pray that good will come to him. You were
called to do this so you might receive good things from God.
1 PETER 3:9

She opens her mouth with wisdom.
The teaching of kindness is on her tongue.
PROVERBS 31:26

God has chosen you. You are holy and loved by Him.
Because of this, your new life should be full of loving-
pity. You should be kind to others and have no pride.
Be gentle and be willing to wait for others.
COLOSSIANS 3:12

As you live God-like, be kind to Christian brothers and love
them. If you have all these things and keep growing in them,
they will keep you from being of no use and from having
no fruit when it comes to knowing our Lord Jesus Christ.
2 PETER 1:7–8

"The Lord of All said, 'Do what is right and be kind and
show loving-pity to one another. Do not make it hard for
the woman whose husband has died, or the child who
has no parents, or the stranger, or the poor. Do not make
sinful plans in your hearts against one another.' "
ZECHARIAH 7:9–10

Each of us should live to please his neighbor.
This will help him grow in faith.
ROMANS 15:2

Be happy with those who are happy.
Be sad with those who are sad.
ROMANS 12:15

Because of this, we should do good to everyone. For sure, we should do good to those who belong to Christ.
GALATIANS 6:10

He who hates his neighbor sins, but happy is he who shows loving-favor to the poor.
PROVERBS 14:21

Give to any person who asks you for something. Do not say no to the man who wants to use something of yours.
MATTHEW 5:42

A Jewish religious leader is weak in many ways because he is just a man himself. He knows how to be gentle with those who know little. He knows how to help those who are doing wrong.
HEBREWS 5:2

And Boaz said, "May the Lord bring good to you, my daughter. You have shown your last kindness to be better than your first by not going after young men, with or without riches. Now my daughter, do not be afraid. I will do for you whatever you ask. For all my people in the city know that you are a good woman.
RUTH 3:10–11

• •

Let no one ever come to you without leaving better and happier. Be the living expression of God's kindness: kindness in your face, kindness in your eyes, kindness in your smile.
MOTHER TERESA

Love of God

Do you love God? Some would think that a trick question. Of course every Christian loves God! Don't they?

The following scriptures address this subject. They tell us that if we love God we will—among other things—seek Him and keep His commandments. Placing God first and desiring His will above our own demonstrates our love and devotion to the One who has done, and continues to do, so much for us.

Loving God is more than lip service, it's God-service.

The Lord takes care of all who love Him.
But He will destroy all the sinful.
PSALM 145:20

"Know then that the Lord your God is God, the faithful
God. He keeps His promise and shows His loving-
kindness to those who love Him and keep His Laws,
even to a thousand family groups in the future."
DEUTERONOMY 7:9

Jesus said to them, "If God were your father,
you would love Me. I came from God. I did
not come on My own, but God sent Me."
JOHN 8:42

God always does what is right. He will not forget the work
you did to help the Christians and the work you are still
doing to help them. This shows your love for Christ.
HEBREWS 6:10

"You must love the Lord your God with all your heart
and with all your soul and with all your strength."
DEUTERONOMY 6:5

Do not love the world or anything in the world. If anyone
loves the world, the Father's love is not in him.
1 JOHN 2:15

I love those who love me, and those who look
for me with much desire will find me.
PROVERBS 8:17

Be happy in the Lord. And He will give
you the desires of your heart.
PSALM 37:4

"Be very careful to love the Lord your God."
JOSHUA 23:11

We know that God makes all things work together for the good
of those who love Him and are chosen to be a part of His plan.
ROMANS 8:28

Keep yourselves in the love of God. Wait for
life that lasts forever through the loving-
kindness of our Lord Jesus Christ.
JUDE 1:21

We have come to know and believe the love God has for us.
God is love. If you live in love, you live by the help of God
and God lives in you. Love is made perfect in us when we
are not ashamed as we stand before Him on the day He
judges. For we know that our life in this world is His life
lived in us. There is no fear in love. Perfect love puts fear
out of our hearts. People have fear when they are afraid
of being punished. The man who is afraid does not have
perfect love. We love Him because He loved us first.
1 JOHN 4:16–19

"The one who loves Me is the one who has My teach-
ing and obeys it. My Father will love whoever loves
Me. I will love him and will show Myself to him."
JOHN 14:21

. . . .

The greatest need in the world today is love. . .
More love for each other and more love for God above!
HELEN STEINER RICE

104

Love for Others

God commands us to love others, and guess what? That includes our enemies too.

It's easy to love those who love us or—at the very least—to love those who are somewhat lovable. But our enemies?

Enemy is a strong word, but you get the picture. It describes anyone who is hostile or adversarial toward you. Like the coworker who diminishes your job position while aggrandizing hers. Or the neighbor who persistently gossips about you despite your efforts to help her.

God's love compels us to love, forgive, understand, and pray for one another. . .even the unlovable.

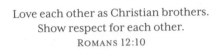

Love each other as Christian brothers.
Show respect for each other.
ROMANS 12:10

You do not need anyone to write to you about loving your
Christian brothers. God has taught you to love each other.
1 THESSALONIANS 4:9

You obey the whole Law when you do this one thing,
"Love your neighbor as you love yourself."
GALATIANS 5:14

As you live God-like, be kind to
Christian brothers and love them.
2 PETER 1:7

Dear friends, if God loved us that much, then
we should love each other. No person has ever
seen God at any time. If we love each other,
God lives in us. His love is made perfect in us.
1 JOHN 4:11–12

And now we have these three: faith and hope
and love, but the greatest of these is love.
1 CORINTHIANS 13:13

"Do not hurt someone who has hurt you. Do not
keep on hating the sons of your people, but love
your neighbor as yourself. I am the Lord."
LEVITICUS 19:18

Do not owe anyone anything, but love each other. Whoever loves his neighbor has done what the Law says to do.
ROMANS 13:8

You may make the weak Christian fall into sin by what
you have done. Remember, he is a Christian brother for
whom Christ died. When you sin against a weak Christian
by making him do what is wrong, you sin against Christ.
1 CORINTHIANS 8:11–12

Let us help each other to love others and to do good.
HEBREWS 10:24

This is the way you can know who are the children
of God and who are the children of the devil. The
person who does not keep on doing what is right and
does not love his brother does not belong to God.
1 JOHN 3:10

If a person says, "I love God," but hates his brother, he is a
liar. If a person does not love his brother whom he has seen,
how can he love God Whom he has not seen? We have these
words from Him. If you love God, love your brother also."
1 JOHN 4:20–21

"Leave your gift on the altar. Go and make right what is wrong
between you and him. Then come back and give your gift."
MATTHEW 5:24

You have made your souls pure by obeying the truth
through the Holy Spirit. This has given you a true love
for the Christians. Let it be a true love from the heart.
1 PETER 1:22

"I give you a new Law. You are to love each other. You
must love each other as I have loved you. If you love
each other, all men will know you are My followers."
JOHN 13:34–35

Last of all, you must share the same thoughts and
the same feelings. Love each other with a kind
heart and with a mind that has no pride.
1 PETER 3:8

. . . .

If I put my own good name before the other's highest
good, then I know nothing of Calvary love.
AMY CARMICHAEL

Meekness

How can a type A lady, with an exuberant, take-charge, outgoing personality, exhibit meekness?

Wouldn't that contradict who she really is?

Jesus not only encourages meekness in His beatitudes, He said "I am gentle and do not have pride" (Matthew 11:29). Yet Jesus was no pushover.

Meekness isn't our outward behavior, but an inwrought grace of the soul. It is a tempered spirit fully surrendered to God, one that accepts His dealings without dispute or resistance. Meekness demonstrates full devotion to and humility before God.

Jesus said that the meek will inherit the earth. And that includes type A personalities too.

Those who suffer will eat and have enough. Those who look for the Lord will praise Him. May your heart live forever!
PSALM 22:26

Great is our Lord, and great in power. His understanding has no end. The Lord lifts up those who are suffering, and He brings the sinful down to the ground.
PSALM 147:5–6

Those who have suffered will be happier in the Lord. Those who are in need will have joy in the Holy One of Israel.
ISAIAH 29:19

Wives, obey your own husbands. Some of your husbands may not obey the Word of God. By obeying your husbands, they may become Christians by the life you live without you saying anything . . . Do not let your beauty come from the outside. It should not be the way you comb your hair or the wearing of gold or the wearing of fine clothes. Your beauty should come from the inside. It should come from the heart. This is the kind that lasts. Your beauty should be a gentle and quiet spirit. In God's sight this is of great worth and no amount of money can buy it.
1 PETER 3:1, 3–4

Look for the Lord, all you people of the earth who are not proud, and who have obeyed His Laws. Look for what is right and good. Have no pride. You may be kept safe on the day of the Lord's anger.
ZEPHANIAH 2:3

"Those who have no pride in their hearts are happy, because the earth will be given to them."
MATTHEW 5:5

Good and right is the Lord. So He teaches sinners in His ways. He leads those without pride into what is right, and teaches them His way.
PSALM 25:8–9

Follow My teachings and learn from Me. I am gentle and do not have pride. You will have rest for your souls.
MATTHEW 11:29

Christian brothers, if a person is found doing some sin, you who are stronger Christians should lead that one back into the right way. Do not be proud as you do it. Watch yourself, because you may be tempted also. Help each other in troubles and problems. This is the kind of law Christ asks us to obey.
GALATIANS 6:1–2

For the Lord is happy with His people. He saves those who have no pride and makes them beautiful.
PSALM 149:4

• •

We can do no great things; only small things with great love.
MOTHER TERESA

Mercy

God is merciful. If He wasn't, most of us would be in big trouble! The Greek translation of *mercy* means "an outward manifestation of pity; it assumes need on the part of him who receives it, and the resources adequate to meet the need on the part of him who shows it." If we love when wronged, we show mercy. If we give or forgive despite our grievances, we exhibit mercy. And if we understand those who are misunderstood, we are merciful. Teamed with goodness, mercy shall follow believers all the days of their lives (Psalm 23:6). Lord, have mercy!

"You must have loving-kindness just as
your Father has loving-kindness."
Luke 6:36

But You, O Lord, are a God full of love and pity. You are
slow to anger and rich in loving-kindness and truth.
Psalm 86:15

So return to your God. Show kindness and do what
is fair, and wait for your God all the time.
Hosea 12:6

"Those who show loving-kindness are happy, because
they will have loving-kindness shown to them."
Matthew 5:7

We think of those who stayed true to Him as happy
even though they suffered. You have heard how long
Job waited. You have seen what the Lord did for him in
the end. The Lord is full of loving-kindness and pity.
James 5:11

For You are good and ready to forgive, O Lord. You
are rich in loving-kindness to all who call to You.
Psalm 86:5

O man, He has told you what is good. What does the
Lord ask of you but to do what is fair and to love kind-
ness, and to walk without pride with your God?
Micah 6:8

God has said that all men have broken His Law.
But He will show loving-kindness on all of them.
Romans 11:32

The Lord is good to all. And His
loving-kindness is over all His works.
Psalm 145:9

Loving-kindness and truth have met together. Peace
and what is right and good have kissed each other.
Psalm 85:10

Do not let kindness and truth leave you. Tie them around your neck. Write them upon your heart. So you will find favor and good understanding in the eyes of God and man.
PROVERBS 3:3–4

It will not go well for the man who hides his sins, but he who tells his sins and turns from them will be given loving-pity.
PROVERBS 28:13

But God had so much loving-kindness. He loved us with such a great love. Even when we were dead because of our sins, He made us alive by what Christ did for us. You have been saved from the punishment of sin by His loving-favor.
EPHESIANS 2:4–5

Let the sinful turn from his way, and the one who does not know God turn from his thoughts. Let him turn to the Lord, and He will have loving-pity on him. Let him turn to our God, for He will for sure forgive all his sins.
ISAIAH 55:7

"I will show loving-kindness to them and forgive their sins. I will remember their sins no more." When God spoke about a New Way of Worship, He showed that the Old Way of Worship was finished and of no use now. It will never be used again.
HEBREWS 8:12–13

"The loving-kindness of the Lord is given to the people of all times who honor Him."
LUKE 1:50

For sure, You will give me goodness and loving-kindness all the days of my life. Then I will live with You in Your house forever.
PSALM 23:6

• •

God deals with us from a merciful posture;
His arms are open, His words are healing,
He wants sinners to return to Him.
MARTIE STOWELL

Modesty

What is true modesty? Current fashions often expose too much skin or fit too tightly, but God's Word tells every woman to dress appropriately. What we wear and how we wear it matters to God because it reflects our inner character and spirit.

Modesty, however, goes far beyond the superficial. A modest spirit is clothed in humility and holiness. A woman who exhibits modesty is not boastful—rather, she seasons her words with kindness and grace. Doing otherwise brings her more embarrassment than wearing her pajamas in public!

Christian women should not be dressed in the kind of clothes and their hair should not be combed in a way that will make people look at them. They should not wear much gold or pearls or clothes that cost much money. Instead of these things, Christian women should be known for doing good things and living good lives.
1 TIMOTHY 2:9–10

Do not fool yourself. If anyone thinks he knows a lot about the things of this world, he had better become a fool. Then he may become wise.
1 CORINTHIANS 3:18

A man's pride will bring him down, but he whose spirit is without pride will receive honor.
PROVERBS 29:23

. . . .

A woman with a gentle and quiet spirit is not only precious to God, but she is attractive to others also. She dresses appropriately, but it is her inner adornment that is noted because she is secure and at rest within her spirit.
CYNTHIA HEALD

Obedience

Elisabeth Elliot, wife of martyred missionary Jim Elliot, said: "God is God. Because He is God, He is worthy of my trust and obedience."

A successful Christian walk is based on our obedience to Christ. In fact, to obey God is to love, serve, trust, and believe Him.

Consider how it pleases you when your child obeys you without question or resistance. He or she simply trusts you at your word and does what you ask. Nice, huh? The same is true of our heavenly Father. It pleases Him when we trust Him enough to obey.

"Now then, if you will obey My voice and keep
My agreement, you will belong to Me from
among all nations. For all the earth is Mine."
EXODUS 19:5

"Be careful to listen to all these words I am telling
you. Then it will go well with you and your children
after you forever. For you will be doing what is good
and right in the eyes of the Lord your God."
DEUTERONOMY 12:28

"Keep His Laws which I am giving you today. Then it may go
well with you and your children after you. And you may live
long in the land the Lord your God is giving you for all time."
DEUTERONOMY 4:40

My son, do not forget my teaching. Let your
heart keep my words. For they will add to you
many days and years of life and peace.
PROVERBS 3:1–2

But the one who keeps looking into God's perfect
Law and does not forget it will do what it says and be
happy as he does it. God's Word makes men free.
JAMES 1:25

Keep on doing all the things you learned and received
and heard from me. Do the things you saw me do.
Then the God Who gives peace will be with you.
PHILIPPIANS 4:9

"If they hear and serve Him, the rest of their days will be
filled with what they need and their years with peace."
JOB 36:11

"Not everyone who says to me, 'Lord, Lord,' will
go into the holy nation of heaven. The one who
does the things My Father in heaven wants him to
do will go into the holy nation of heaven."
MATTHEW 7:21

"I tell you today to love the Lord your God. Walk in His ways. Keep all His Laws and all that He has decided. Then you will live and become many. And the Lord your God will bring good to you in the land you are going in to take."
DEUTERONOMY 30:16

The last word, after all has been heard, is: Honor God and obey His Laws. This is all that every person must do.
ECCLESIASTES 12:13

"If you obey My teaching, you will live in My love. In this way, I have obeyed My Father's teaching and live in His love."
JOHN 15:10

"Anyone who breaks even the least of the Law of Moses and teaches people not to do what it says, will be called the least in the holy nation of heaven. He who obeys and teaches others to obey what the Law of Moses says, will be called great in the holy nation of heaven."
MATTHEW 5:19

Just to hear the Law does not make a man right with God. The man right with God is the one who obeys the Law.
ROMANS 2:13

The world and all its desires will pass away. But the man who obeys God and does what He wants done will live forever.
1 JOHN 2:17

But He said, "Yes, but those who hear the Word of God and obey it are happy."
LUKE 11:28

"So be careful to keep the words of this
agreement and obey them so that all will go well."
DEUTERONOMY 29:9

Happy are those who keep His Law and
look for Him with all their heart.
PSALM 119:2

Remember that our fathers on earth punished us.
We had respect for them. How much more should
we obey our Father in heaven and live?
HEBREWS 12:9

My Christian friends, you have obeyed me when I was with
you. You have obeyed even more when I have been away. You
must keep on working to show you have been saved from the
punishment of sin. Be afraid that you may not please God.
PHILIPPIANS 2:12

"If you are willing and obey, you will eat the best of the land."
ISAIAH 1:19

• •

The only way I will keep a pliable, obedient
spirit in the larger decisions is to look to
Him and to obey in the smaller ones.
CATHERINE MARSHALL

Patience

Patience is a lost virtue in today's fast-paced, I-want-it-now society. We want results and we want them immediately! Just ask any woman on a diet. After a week or so, some of us fall off the wagon when the number on the scale doesn't drop quickly enough.

Our impatience surfaces in other ways too— everything from waiting in a store checkout line to waiting for answered prayer.

Attaining patience is a process, often birthed from endurance on the battlefield of trials. Yet patience is a virtue worth working— and waiting—for.

A servant owned by God must not make trouble.
He must be kind to everyone. He must be able to teach.
He must be willing to suffer when hurt for doing good.
2 TIMOTHY 2:24

You must be willing to wait without giving up.
After you have done what God wants you to do,
God will give you what He promised you.
HEBREWS 10:36

You know these prove your faith. It helps you not
to give up. Learn well how to wait so you will be
strong and complete and in need of nothing.
JAMES 1:3–4

"But those which fell on good ground have heard
the Word. They keep it in a good and true heart
and they keep on giving good grain."
LUKE 8:15

"This is why God's people need to keep true
to God's Word and stay faithful to Jesus."
REVELATION 14:12

May the Lord lead your hearts into the love of
God. May He help you as you wait for Christ.
2 THESSALONIANS 3:5

"But stay true and your souls will have life."
LUKE 21:19

"Christian brothers, be willing to wait for the Lord to
come again. Learn from the farmer. He waits for the
good fruit from the earth until the early and late rains
come. You must be willing to wait also. Be strong in
your hearts because the Lord is coming again soon."
JAMES 5:7–8

All these many people who have had faith in God are around us like a cloud. Let us put every thing out of our lives that keeps us from doing what we should. Let us keep running in the race that God has planned for us.
HEBREWS 12:1

Do not be lazy. Be like those who have faith and have not given up. They will receive what God has promised them.
HEBREWS 6:12

What good is it if, when you are beaten for doing something wrong, you do not try to get out of it? But if you are beaten when you have done what is right, and do not try to get out of it, God is pleased.
1 PETER 2:20

The end of something is better than its beginning. Not giving up in spirit is better than being proud in spirit. Do not be quick in spirit to be angry. For anger is in the heart of fools.
ECCLESIASTES 7:8–9

Abraham was willing to wait and God gave to him what He had promised.
HEBREWS 6:15

Those who keep on doing good and are looking for His greatness and honor will receive life that lasts forever.
ROMANS 2:7

· ·

Obedience is the fruit of faith;
patience, the bloom on the fruit.
CHRISTINA ROSSETTI

122

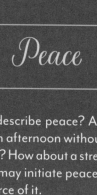

Peace

How do you describe peace? A day spent at the beach? An afternoon without phone calls and to-do lists? How about a stress-free week? Those things may initiate peace, but they are rarely the source of it.

God gives us a peace that surpasses human understanding—the kind of peace that prevails in the most difficult situations or alarming circumstances. Only the Lord can administer tranquility in the midst of life's storms.

Need peace? Relax and bask in the peace that only God provides.

Our hope comes from God. May He fill you with joy
and peace because of your trust in Him. May your hope
grow stronger by the power of the Holy Spirit.
ROMANS 15:13

The Lord will give strength to His people.
The Lord will give His people peace.
PSALM 29:11

When the ways of a man are pleasing to the Lord, He
makes even those who hate him to be at peace with him.
PROVERBS 16:7

"Those who make peace are happy,
because they will be called the sons of God."
MATTHEW 5:9

Lying is in the heart of those who plan what is
bad, but those who plan peace have joy.
PROVERBS 12:20

Those who plant seeds of peace will
gather what is right and good.
JAMES 3:18

As much as you can, live in peace with all men.
ROMANS 12:18

The peace of God is much greater than the human
mind can understand. This peace will keep your
hearts and minds through Christ Jesus.
PHILIPPIANS 4:7

You must think much of them and love them because
of their work. Live in peace with each other.
1 THESSALONIANS 5:13

First of all, I ask you to pray much for all men and to give thanks for them. Pray for kings and all others who are in power over us so we might live quiet God-like lives in peace.
1 TIMOTHY 2:1–2

Be at peace with all men. Live a holy life. No one will see the Lord without having that kind of life.
HEBREWS 12:14

See, how good and how pleasing it is for brothers to live together as one!
PSALM 133:1

For "If you want joy in your life and have happy days, keep your tongue from saying bad things and your lips from talking bad about others. Turn away from what is sinful. Do what is good. Look for peace and go after it."
1 PETER 3:10–11

"You will keep the man in perfect peace whose mind is kept on You, because he trusts in You."
ISAIAH 26:3

For God did not give us a spirit of fear. He gave us a spirit of power and of love and of a good mind.
2 TIMOTHY 1:7

. . . .

When the presence of the Lord really becomes your experience, you will actually discover that you have gradually begun to love this silence and peaceful rest which come with His presence.
MADAME GUYON

Perseverance

You've tried everything to no avail. Now what? You've prayed for a loved one for years, but nothing changes. What do you do?

The Lord tells us that after we've done everything we know to do, and have said everything we know to say, to stand. In other words, persevere. Keep believing, praying, and standing in faith.

The same holds true for every area of our lives. We must hold steady in the face of adversity, doubt, or apparent failure. Why? Because God is faithful if we will only stand fast and persevere against all odds.

For this reason, I am suffering. But I am not ashamed. I know the One in Whom I have put my trust. I am sure He is able to keep safe that which I have trusted to Him until the day He comes again. Keep all the things I taught you. They were given to you in the faith and love of Jesus Christ.
2 TIMOTHY 1:12–13

"You have ears! Then listen to what the Spirit says to the churches. The person who has power and wins will not be hurt by the second death!"
REVELATION 2:11

For we belong to Christ if we keep on trusting Him to the end just as we trusted Him at first.
HEBREWS 3:14

"I will allow the one who has power and wins to sit with Me on My throne, as I also had power and won and sat down with My Father on His throne."
REVELATION 3:21

These tests have come to prove your faith and to show that it is good. Gold, which can be destroyed, is tested by fire. Your faith is worth much more than gold and it must be tested also. Then your faith will bring thanks and shining-greatness and honor to Jesus Christ when He comes again.
1 PETER 1:7

Take your share of suffering as a good soldier of Jesus Christ.
2 TIMOTHY 2:3

When he falls, he will not be thrown down, because the Lord holds his hand.
PSALM 37:24

Let us hold on to the hope we say we have and not be changed. We can trust God that He will do what He promised.
HEBREWS 10:23

For I know that nothing can keep us from the love of God. Death cannot! Life cannot! Angels cannot! Leaders cannot! Any other power cannot! Hard things now or in the future cannot! The world above or the world below cannot! Any other living thing cannot keep us away from the love of God which is ours through Christ Jesus our Lord.

ROMANS 8:38–39

Christ made us free. Stay that way. Do not get chained all over again in the Law and its kind of religious worship.

GALATIANS 5:1

But the way of those who are right is like the early morning light. It shines brighter and brighter until the perfect day.

PROVERBS 4:18

He said to the Jews who believed, "If you keep and obey My Word, then you are My followers for sure."

JOHN 8:31

And so, dear friends, now that you know this, watch so you will not be led away by the mistakes of these sinful people. Do not be moved by them.

2 PETER 3:17

Who can keep us away from the love of Christ? Can trouble or problems? Can suffering wrong from others or having no food? Can it be because of no clothes or because of danger or war?

ROMANS 8:35

Because of this, put on all the things God gives you to fight with. Then you will be able to stand in that sinful day. When it is all over, you will still be standing.

EPHESIANS 6:13

• •

You may have to fight a battle more than once to win it.

MARGARET THATCHER

Power

Workshops, conferences, books, and magazines all herald the attributes of *empowerment* and what it can mean in a woman's life. We long to fortify ourselves with the knowledge, wisdom, capabilities, and tools that will give us the power to become or do something greater than ourselves.

The scriptures talk a lot about power too—the power of God. As the Lord empowers us through the Holy Spirit, we change in ways we never dreamed and accomplish the seemingly impossible with His help. The truth is, self-empowerment often fades into futility, but God's power empowers the powerless continually.

Look to the Lord and ask for His strength.
Look to Him all the time.
1 Chronicles 16:11

"The Lord your God is with you, a Powerful One
Who wins the battle. He will have much joy over
you. With His love He will give you new life. He
will have joy over you with loud singing."
Zephaniah 3:17

God is able to do much more than we ask or
think through His power working in us.
Ephesians 3:20

The holy nation of God is not made up of
words. It is made up of power.
1 Corinthians 4:20

. . . .

The stone still stood there in that quiet garden, a
reminder of the reality of the problem we all must live
with; but Christ had moved it to one side so very easily,
demonstrating His resurrection power on our behalf.
JILL BRISCOE

Prayer

A mother prays for her child at the foot of a tearstained bed. An elderly woman sits in a wheelchair interceding for her church. A grandmother kneels at the kitchen sink to pray for her grandchildren. A young woman sits in a classroom, whispering a prayer for a friend, and a little girl places her hand on her sick puppy and prays.

Prayer is simply talking to God. Lofty words and pious phrases are unnecessary—only a pure, honest, and sincere heart matters. God's power is unleashed through prayer. So pray often, anywhere, anytime.

"When the time comes that you see Me again, you will ask Me no question. For sure, I tell you, My Father will give you whatever you ask in My name. Until now you have not asked for anything in My name. Ask and you will receive. Then your joy will be full."
JOHN 16:23–24

"When you pray, go into a room by yourself. After you have shut the door, pray to your Father Who is in secret. Then your Father Who sees in secret will reward you. When you pray, do not say the same thing over and over again making long prayers like the people who do not know God. They think they are heard because their prayers are long."
MATTHEW 6:6–7

Hear my words, O Lord. Think about my crying. Listen to my cry for help, my King and my God. For I pray to you.
PSALM 5:1–2

"Then we will use all of our time to pray and to teach the Word of God."
ACTS 6:4

"You are bad and you know how to give good things to your children. How much more will your Father in heaven give good things to those who ask Him?"
MATTHEW 7:11

Be happy in your hope. Do not give up when trouble comes. Do not let anything stop you from praying.
ROMANS 12:12

"If My people who are called by My name put away their pride and pray, and look for My face, and turn from their sinful ways, then I will hear from heaven. I will forgive their sin, and will heal their land."
2 CHRONICLES 7:14

You will pray to Him, and He will hear you.
And you will keep your promises to Him.
JOB 22:27

You must pray at all times as the Holy Spirit leads you to
pray. Pray for the things that are needed. You must watch
and keep on praying. Remember to pray for all Christians.
EPHESIANS 6:18

I did not give up waiting for the Lord.
And He turned to me and heard my cry.
PSALM 40:1

"Will not God make the things that are right come
to His chosen people who cry day and night to
Him? Will He wait a long time to help them?"
LUKE 18:7

"Then you will call upon Me and come and pray to Me,
and I will listen to you. You will look for Me and find
Me, when you look for Me with all your heart."
JEREMIAH 29:12–13

"All things you ask for in prayer,
you will receive if you have faith."
MATTHEW 21:22

The Lord is near to all who call on Him,
to all who call on Him in truth.
PSALM 145:18

Let us go with complete trust to the throne of God.
We will receive His loving-kindness and have His
loving-favor to help us whenever we need it.
HEBREWS 4:16

The Lord hates the gifts of the sinful,
but the prayer of the faithful is His joy.
PROVERBS 15:8

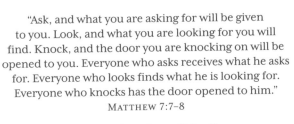

"Ask, and what you are asking for will be given
to you. Look, and what you are looking for you will
find. Knock, and the door you are knocking on will be
opened to you. Everyone who asks receives what he asks
for. Everyone who looks finds what he is looking for.
Everyone who knocks has the door opened to him."
MATTHEW 7:7–8

"And it will be before they call, I will answer.
While they are still speaking, I will hear."
ISAIAH 65:24

Tell your sins to each other. And pray for each other
so you may be healed. The prayer from the heart
of a man right with God has much power.
JAMES 5:16

I want men everywhere to pray. They should lift up holy
hands as they pray. They should not be angry or argue.
1 TIMOTHY 2:8

Let them give thanks to the Lord for His loving-
kindness and His great works to the children of men!
PSALM 107:15

So they caused the cry of the poor to come to
Him. And He heard the cry of those in need.
JOB 34:28

What should I do? I will pray with my spirit and
I will pray with my mind also. I will sing with my
spirit and I will sing with my mind also.
1 CORINTHIANS 14:15

The Lord will send His loving-kindness in
the day. And His song will be with me in the
night, a prayer to the God of my life.
PSALM 42:8

Never stop praying.
1 THESSALONIANS 5:17

"Again I tell you this: If two of you agree on earth about
anything you pray for, it will be done for you by My
Father in heaven. For where two or three are gathered together in My name, there I am with them."
MATTHEW 18:19–20

He will call upon Me, and I will answer him. I will be with him
in trouble. I will take him out of trouble and honor him.
PSALM 91:15

I will call on Him as long as I live, because
He has turned His ear to me.
PSALM 116:2

. . . .

Prayer is an indispensable part of our
relationship with Jesus Christ.
LAUREL OKE LOGAN

Pride

Have you noticed that boasting has become an admirable attribute? (To clarify: Confidence in one's abilities or talents is different from bragging about them.) With much bravado, women from the boardroom to the catwalk herald their gifts and talents with more intensity than an on-the-scene journalist broadcasting breaking news.

Pride is not only admissible in the world, it's expected. To God, however, pride is sin. A proud and haughty spirit is unattractive and unacceptable to the King of kings. Besides, any king's daughter would rather brag about her heavenly Father's attributes than about her own.

Do not be wise in your own eyes. Fear the Lord
and turn away from what is sinful.
PROVERBS 3:7

Jesus sat down and called the followers to Him.
He said, "If anyone wants to be first, he must be
last of all. He will be the one to care for all."
MARK 9:35

"For sure God will not listen to an empty cry.
The All-powerful will not do anything about it."
JOB 35:13

Eyes lifted high and a proud heart is sin
and is the lamp of the sinful.
PROVERBS 21:4

But instead you are proud. You talk loud and
big about yourselves. All such pride is sin.
JAMES 4:16

Live in peace with each other. Do not act or think
with pride. Be happy to be with poor people. Keep
yourself from thinking you are so wise.
ROMANS 12:16

"Speak no more in your pride. Do not let proud
talk come out of your mouth. For the Lord is a
God Who knows. Actions are weighed by Him."
1 SAMUEL 2:3

The fear of the Lord is to hate what is sinful.
I hate pride, self-love, the way of sin, and lies.
PROVERBS 8:13

If anyone wants to be proud, he should be proud of what
the Lord has done. It is not what a man thinks and says of
himself that is important. It is what God thinks of him.
2 CORINTHIANS 10:17–18

"How can you believe when you are always wanting
honor from each other? And yet you do not look
for the honor that comes from the only God."
JOHN 5:44

Pride comes before being destroyed and
a proud spirit comes before a fall.
PROVERBS 16:18

God has given me His loving-favor. This helps me write
these things to you. I ask each one of you not to think more
of himself than he should think. Instead, think in the right
way toward yourself by the faith God has given you.
ROMANS 12:3

If anyone thinks he is important when he
is nothing, he is fooling himself.
GALATIANS 6:3

• •

Why are we not far more frightened of what pride can
do? Pride can cost us—and probably those after us.
BETH MOORE

Protection

As women, we walk with caution to our car or on the street at night. We warn our daughters to guard themselves against possible intruders or attacks. Mothers use child-safety products to protect toddlers from harm, and we teach our children to avoid strangers and to look both ways before crossing the street.

Similarly, God protects us. He provides a refuge in life's storms with the assurance that He is with us in every situation. He takes extra precaution to guide, assist, instruct, and protect us each day. He is our help, our shield, and our best protection.

The Lord of All is with us. The God of Jacob is our strong place.
PSALM 46:7

There is strong trust in the fear of the Lord,
and His children will have a safe place.
PROVERBS 14:26

"When you pass through the waters, I will be with
you. When you pass through the rivers, they will not
flow over you. When you walk through the fire, you
will not be burned. The fire will not destroy you."
ISAIAH 43:2

But the Lord has been my strong place,
my God, and the rock where I am safe.
PSALM 94:22

Be a rock to me where I live, where I may always come and
where I will be safe. For You are my rock and my safe place.
PSALM 71:3

Most important of all, you need a covering of faith in front
of you. This is to put out the fire-arrows of the devil.
EPHESIANS 6:16

For You will make those happy who do what is right,
O Lord. You will cover them all around with Your favor.
PSALM 5:12

The name of the Lord is a strong tower. The man
who does what is right runs into it and is safe.
PROVERBS 18:10

Our soul waits for the Lord. He is our help and our safe cover.
PSALM 33:20

Every word of God has been proven true.
He is a safe-covering to those who trust in Him.
PROVERBS 30:5

He will cover you with His wings. And under His wings you will be safe. He is faithful like a safe-covering and a strong wall.
PSALM 91:4

"But he who listens to me will live free from danger, and he will rest easy from the fear of what is sinful."
PROVERBS 1:33

For You are my rock and my safe place. For the honor of Your name, lead me and show me the way.
PSALM 31:3

The Lord is good, a safe place in times of trouble. And He knows those who come to Him to be safe.
NAHUM 1:7

Give all your cares to the Lord and He will give you strength. He will never let those who are right with Him be shaken.
PSALM 55:22

"The God Who lives forever is your safe place. His arms are always under you. He drove away from in front of you those who hate you, and said,'Destroy!' "
DEUTERONOMY 33:27

The Lord also keeps safe those who suffer. He is a safe place in times of trouble.
PSALM 9:9

God is our safe place and our strength. He is always our help when we are in trouble.
PSALM 46:1

· ·

God will never lead you where His strength cannot keep you.
BARBARA JOHNSON

Purity

Christians take heart. Purity is gaining popularity. Teenagers across the country are vowing abstinence by wearing "purity rings." The silver band symbolizes a teen's vow to celibacy until marriage—it is an expression of his or her love and commitment to God and the promise to live a pure life. Whether we are fourteen or fifty, the pledge to purity can begin anytime and carry throughout our lifetime. God calls every believer to a life of holiness without fornication, adultery, or impurity. A pure life is a fully consecrated one, with or without a symbolic ring.

Drink water from your own pool,
flowing water from your own well.
PROVERBS 5:15

Destroy the desires to sin that are in you. These
desires are: sex sins, anything that is not clean,
a desire for sex sins, and wanting something
someone else has. This is worshiping a god. It is
because of these sins that the anger of God
comes down on those who do not obey Him.
COLOSSIANS 3:5–6

Do not let sex sins or anything sinful be even
talked about among those who belong to
Christ. Do not always want everything.
EPHESIANS 5:3

"Do not do sex sins."
EXODUS 20:14

· ·

A person of purity stands before his peers
and superiors and courageously
maintains his faith in God.
CINDY TRENT

Repentance

What is repentance? To regret you bought those expensive shoes? To wish you hadn't opened your mouth, or to kick yourself for not speaking up?

To *repent* means to change one's mind, yes. But it also means to turn *away* from sin and turn *toward* God. The Lord cannot forgive us of our sins until we repent of them and turn to Him for salvation.

Did you know that there is a good kind of sorrow? It's the sorrow that leads us to repentance (2 Corinthians 7:10). As we repent, God forgives and our new life begins.

The sorrow that God uses makes people sorry for their sin and leads them to turn from sin so they can be saved from the punishment of sin. We should be happy for that kind of sorrow, but the sorrow of this world brings death.

2 Corinthians 7:10

The Lord is not slow about keeping His promise as some people think. He is waiting for you. The Lord does not want any person to be punished forever. He wants all people to be sorry for their sins and turn from them.

2 Peter 3:9

"God did not remember these times when people did not know better. But now He tells all men everywhere to be sorry for their sins and to turn from them."

Acts 17:30

"But go and understand these words, 'I want loving-kindness and not a gift to be given.' For I have not come to call good people. I have come to call those who are sinners."

Matthew 9:13

"So remember what you have received and heard. Keep it. Be sorry for your sins and turn from them. If you will not wake up, I will come as a robber. You will not know at what time I will come."

Revelation 3:3

Do you forget about His loving-kindness to you? Do you forget how long He is waiting for you? You know that God is kind. He is trying to get you to be sorry for your sins and turn from them.

Romans 2:4

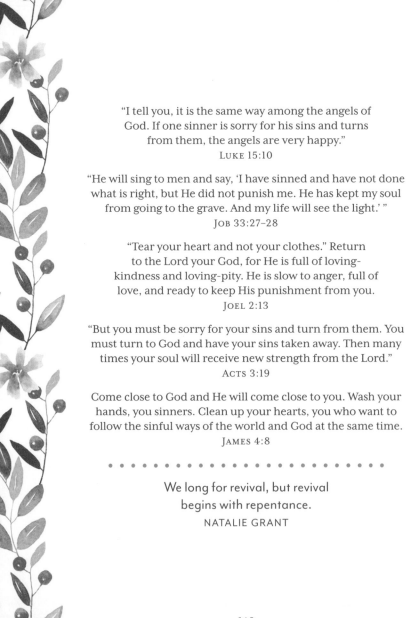

"I tell you, it is the same way among the angels of God. If one sinner is sorry for his sins and turns from them, the angels are very happy."
Luke 15:10

"He will sing to men and say, 'I have sinned and have not done what is right, but He did not punish me. He has kept my soul from going to the grave. And my life will see the light.' "
Job 33:27–28

"Tear your heart and not your clothes." Return to the Lord your God, for He is full of loving-kindness and loving-pity. He is slow to anger, full of love, and ready to keep His punishment from you.
Joel 2:13

"But you must be sorry for your sins and turn from them. You must turn to God and have your sins taken away. Then many times your soul will receive new strength from the Lord."
Acts 3:19

Come close to God and He will come close to you. Wash your hands, you sinners. Clean up your hearts, you who want to follow the sinful ways of the world and God at the same time.
James 4:8

• •

We long for revival, but revival begins with repentance.
NATALIE GRANT

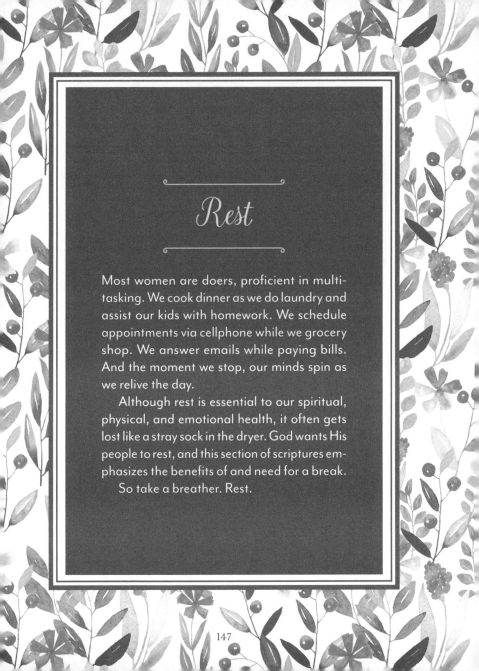

Rest

Most women are doers, proficient in multi-tasking. We cook dinner as we do laundry and assist our kids with homework. We schedule appointments via cellphone while we grocery shop. We answer emails while paying bills. And the moment we stop, our minds spin as we relive the day.

Although rest is essential to our spiritual, physical, and emotional health, it often gets lost like a stray sock in the dryer. God wants His people to rest, and this section of scriptures emphasizes the benefits of and need for a break.

So take a breather. Rest.

I will lie down and sleep in peace.
O Lord, You alone keep me safe.
PSALM 4:8

In the Holy Writings He said this about the seventh day
when He made the whole world, "God rested on the
seventh day from all He had made.". . . And so God's
people have a complete rest waiting for them.
HEBREWS 4:4, 9

"Then you would trust, because there is hope.
You would look around and rest and be safe."
JOB 11:18

He who lives in the safe place of the Most High
will be in the shadow of the All-powerful.
PSALM 91:1

Rest in the Lord and be willing to wait for Him.
Do not trouble yourself when all goes well with
the one who carries out his sinful plans.
PSALM 37:7

• •

Again and again, I've found Him faithful
to respond, and the closer I move to Him,
the safer I feel and the better I rest.
PATSY CLAIRMONT

Righteousness

What is righteousness? What can we do to attain it? Is right living the ticket? Or is there something more we should know or do?

The definition of *righteousness* includes the following: "A quality or character of uprightness; an attribute of God and whatever or whoever conforms to the revealed will of God."

Contrary to what some believe, God's righteousness is only attainable through faith in Christ, not through obedience to a prescribed set of laws or good deeds (Ephesians 2:8–9).

Do you desire righteousness? Accept Christ and follow His Word.

"First of all, look for the holy nation of God. Be right with
Him. All these other things will be given to you also."
MATTHEW 6:33

O Lord, who may live in Your tent? Who may live on Your
holy hill? He who walks without blame and does what
is right and good, and speaks the truth in his heart.
PSALM 15:1–2

"He does not turn His eyes away from those who
are right with Him. He puts them on the throne
with kings and they are honored forever."
JOB 36:7

All of Your Word is truth, and every one of Your
laws, which are always right, will last forever.
PSALM 119:160

"Then the ones right with God will shine as the sun in the
holy nation of their Father. You have ears, then listen!"
MATTHEW 13:43

Those who are right with the Lord cry, and He hears
them. And He takes them from all their troubles.
PSALM 34:17

"But if you obey his voice and do all that I say,
then I will hate those who hate you and fight
against those who fight against you."
EXODUS 23:22

If we tell Him our sins, He is faithful and we
can depend on Him to forgive us of our sins.
He will make our lives clean from all sin.
1 JOHN 1:9

Let those who love the Lord hate what is bad. For He keeps
safe the souls of His faithful ones. He takes them away from
the hand of the sinful. Light is spread like seed for those
who are right and good, and joy for the pure in heart.
PSALM 97:10–11

"Be faithful in obeying the Lord your God. Be careful to keep all His Laws which I tell you today. And the Lord your God will set you high above all the nations of the earth."
DEUTERONOMY 28:1

The Lord will not let those who are right with Him go hungry, but He puts to one side the desire of the sinful.
PROVERBS 10:3

He who follows what is right and loving and kind finds life, right-standing with God and honor.
PROVERBS 21:21

Know that the Lord has set apart him who is God-like for Himself. The Lord hears when I call to Him.
PSALM 4:3

"Then He will say to them, 'For sure, I tell you, because you did not do it to one of the least of these, you did not do it to Me.' These will go to the place where they will be punished forever. But those right with God will have life that lasts forever."
MATTHEW 25:45–46

The man who is right and good will be glad in the Lord and go to Him to be safe. All those whose hearts are right will give Him praise.
PSALM 64:10

Christ never sinned but God put our sin on Him. Then we are made right with God because of what Christ has done for us.
2 CORINTHIANS 5:21

• •

We do not have to be qualified to be holy.
MADELEINE L'ENGLE

Salvation

In the world, work is a prerequisite to achievement. In God's Word, works are meaningless without faith in Christ. Salvation is God's free gift to anyone who confesses her sins and asks Jesus into her heart and life. Why? Because Jesus paid the price for our sins when He died on the cross—and by accepting Him, we are given salvation and eternal life.

Have you asked Jesus into your heart? If not, He stands at your door and knocks. All you need do is invite Him in. Go ahead. He's been waiting awhile.

For if a man belongs to Christ, he is a new person.
The old life is gone. New life has begun.
2 CORINTHIANS 5:17

My dear children, I am writing this to you so you will not sin.
But if anyone does sin, there is One Who will go between
him and the Father. He is Jesus Christ, the One Who is right
with God. He paid for our sins with His own blood. He did
not pay for ours only, but for the sins of the whole world.
1 JOHN 2:1-2

It is good when you pray like this. It pleases God Who is the
One Who saves. He wants all people to be saved from the
punishment of sin. He wants them to come to know the truth.
1 TIMOTHY 2:3-4

He gave the right and the power to become children
of God to those who received Him. He gave this to
those who put their trust in His name. These children
of God were not born of blood and of flesh and of
man's desires, but they were born of God.
JOHN 1:12-13

"He who puts his trust in the Son has life that lasts
forever. He who does not put his trust in the Son
will not have life, but the anger of God is on him."
JOHN 3:36

"There is no way to be saved from the punishment of sin
through anyone else. For there is no other name under
heaven given to men by which we can be saved."
ACTS 4:12

But God, the One Who saves, showed how kind He was and how He loved us by saving us from the punishment of sin. It was not because we worked to be right with God. It was because of His loving-kindness that He washed our sins away. At the same time He gave us new life when the Holy Spirit came into our lives. God gave the Holy Spirit to fill our lives through Jesus Christ, the One Who saves.

TITUS 3:4–6

I want to please everyone in all that I do. I am not thinking of myself. I want to do what is best for them so they may be saved from the punishment of sin.

1 CORINTHIANS 10:33

Jesus said to him, "For sure, I tell you, unless a man is born again, he cannot see the holy nation of God." Nicodemus said to Him, "How can a man be born when he is old? How can he get into his mother's body and be born the second time?" Jesus answered, "For sure, I tell you, unless a man is born of water and of the Spirit of God, he cannot get into the holy nation of God. Whatever is born of the flesh is flesh. Whatever is born of the Spirit is spirit. Do not be surprised that I said to you, 'You must be born again.'"

JOHN 3:3–7

• •

Christ has made all things right. I had nothing to do but accept it as a free gift from Him.

HANNAH WHITALL SMITH

Scripture

Is the Bible just an ancient history book? What significance do the scriptures have in modern society?

As the following verses indicate, the scriptures are the life-giving, soul-sustaining, power-packed, anointed words of God! They provide us with the spiritual nutrients necessary for daily living.

God's Word reveals God's will and character to us, bringing salvation, healing, deliverance, hope, peace, wisdom, guidance, and restoration to those who read its pages.

Just an ancient history book inapplicable to today's lifestyle and issues? Read on.

Let the teaching of Christ and His words keep on
living in you. These make your lives rich and full of
wisdom. Keep on teaching and helping each other.
Sing the Songs of David and the church songs and the
songs of heaven with hearts full of thanks to God.
COLOSSIANS 3:16

Your Word have I hid in my heart,
that I may not sin against You.
PSALM 119:11

You have known the Holy Writings since you
were a child. They are able to give you wisdom
that leads to being saved from the punishment
of sin by putting your trust in Christ Jesus.
2 TIMOTHY 3:15

Your Word is a lamp to my feet and a light to my path.
PSALM 119:105

"Keep these words of mine in your heart and in your
soul. Tie them as something special to see upon your
hand and on your forehead between your eyes. Teach
them to your children. Talk about them when you
sit in your house and when you walk on the road
and when you lie down and when you get up."
DEUTERONOMY 11:18–19

God's Word is living and powerful. It is sharper than
a sword that cuts both ways. It cuts straight into
where the soul and spirit meet and it divides them.
It cuts into the joints and bones. It tells what the
heart is thinking about and what it wants to do.
HEBREWS 4:12

Long ago God spoke to our early fathers in many different ways. He spoke through the early preachers. But in these last days He has spoken to us through His Son. God gave His Son everything. It was by His Son that God made the world.

HEBREWS 1:1–2

"This book of the Law must not leave your mouth. Think about it day and night, so you may be careful to do all that is written in it. Then all will go well with you. You will receive many good things."

JOSHUA 1:8

The early preachers wondered at what time or to what person this would happen. The Spirit of Christ in them was talking to them and told them to write about how Christ would suffer and about His shining-greatness later on. They knew these things would not happen during the time they lived but while you are living many years later. These are the very things that were told to you by those who preached the Good News. The Holy Spirit Who was sent from heaven gave them power and they told of things that even the angels would like to know about.

1 PETER 1:11–12

• •

How much of a calm and gentle spirit you achieve, then, will depend on how regularly and consistently, persistently and obediently you partake of the Word of God, your spiritual food.

SHIRLEY RICE

Seeking God

I once lost my then-small son in an interactive playroom at Disney World. Panic set in as I scoured every area. About to notify security, I raced to the escalator where Jeff stood sobbing. "Where were you?" he whimpered, as if I was the one who was lost.

Similarly, God isn't lost—we are. Our search for Him begins when we realize that. Most of us seek God when we're afraid, discouraged, sick, or sad. But God desires for us to seek Him because we yearn to know Him. These passages reveal how God blesses and rewards those who diligently seek Him.

"First of all, look for the holy nation of God. Be right with Him. All these other things will be given to you also."
MATTHEW 6:33

"Plant what is right and good for yourselves. Gather the fruit of lasting love. Break up your ground that has not been plowed. For it is time to look for the Lord, until He comes and pours His saving power on you."
HOSEA 10:12

"Look to the Lord and ask for His strength. Look to Him all the time."
1 CHRONICLES 16:11

"Have joy in His holy name. Let the heart of those who look to the Lord be glad."
1 CHRONICLES 16:10

"You will look for Me and find Me, when you look for Me with all your heart."
JEREMIAH 29:13

One thing I have asked from the Lord, that I will ook for: that I may live in the house of the Lord all the days of my life, to look upon the beauty of the Lord, and to worship in His holy house.
PSALM 27:4

My soul has a desire for You in the night. Yes, my spirit within me looks for You in the morning. For when you punish the earth, the people of the world learn what is right and good.
ISAIAH 26:9

Look for the Lord and live.
AMOS 5:6

"But from there you will look for the Lord your God. And you
will find Him if you look for Him with all your heart and soul."
DEUTERONOMY 4:29

If then you have been raised with Christ, keep
looking for the good things of heaven. This is
where Christ is seated on the right side of God.
COLOSSIANS 3:1

"Have joy in His holy name. Let the heart
of those who look to the Lord be glad."
1 CHRONICLES 16:10

The young lions suffer want and hunger. But they who
look for the Lord will not be without any good thing.
PSALM 34:10

"If My people who are called by My name put away
their pride and pray, and look for My face, and turn
from their sinful ways, then I will hear from heaven.
I will forgive their sin, and will heal their land."
2 CHRONICLES 7:14

• •

For it is impossible to be in the presence
of Jesus and not be changed.
JOANNA WEAVER

Self-Control

Pastries line the table. "Have one," the hostess says. "Thanks, but I'm dieting," you respond. "One won't hurt," she prods, handing you a chocolate tart. Soon one tart turns into three with a side dish of strawberry cheesecake. "I'll resume my diet tomorrow," you reason, self-control scrambling away faster than rats from a burning building.

When we act, say, go, or do what we shouldn't, we lose control—and end up regretting it. The Bible teaches that self-control and moderation is achievable. Our desires may tempt us, but they don't have to control us. Even while we're dieting!

These things are all a part of the Christian life to which you have been called. Christ suffered for us. This shows us we are to follow in His steps. He never sinned. No lie or bad talk ever came from His lips. When people spoke against Him, He never spoke back. When He suffered from what people did to Him, He did not try to pay them back. He left it in the hands of the One Who is always right in judging.
1 PETER 2:21–23

Have you found honey? Eat only what you need,
or you may become filled with it and spit it up.
PROVERBS 25:16

Love does not give up. Love is kind. Love is not jealous. Love does not put itself up as being important. Love has no pride. Love does not do the wrong thing. Love never thinks of itself. Love does not get angry. Love does not remember the suffering that comes from being hurt by someone.
1 CORINTHIANS 13:4–5

Older men are to be quiet and to be careful how they act. They are to be the boss over their own desires. Their faith and love are to stay strong and they are not to give up.
TITUS 2:2

We must act all the time as if it were day. Keep away from wild parties and do not be drunk. Keep yourself free from sex sins and bad actions. Do not fight or be jealous. Let every part of you belong to the Lord Jesus Christ. Do not allow your weak thoughts to lead you into sinful actions.
ROMANS 13:13–14

Do your best to add holy living to your faith. Then add to this a better understanding. As you have a better understanding, be able to say no when you need to. Do not give up. And as you wait and do not give up, live God-like.
2 PETER 1:5–6

Then Pilate said to Him, "Do You not hear all these things they are saying against You?" Jesus did not say a word. The leader was much surprised and wondered about it.
MATTHEW 27:13–14

Michael was one of the head angels. He argued with the devil about the body of Moses. But Michael would not speak sharp words to the devil, saying he was guilty. He said, "The Lord speaks sharp words to you."
JUDE 1:9

Everyone who runs in a race does many things so his body will be strong. He does it to get a crown that will soon be worth nothing, but we work for a crown that will last forever.
1 CORINTHIANS 9:25

Let him sit alone and be quiet when God has laid the load on him. Let him put his mouth in the dust. There may be hope yet.
LAMENTATIONS 3:28–29

We are taught to have nothing to do with that which is against God. We are to have nothing to do with the desires of this world. We are to be wise and to be right with God. We are to live God-like lives in this world.
TITUS 2:12

If you do what your sinful old selves want you to do, you will die in sin. But if, through the power of the Holy Spirit, you destroy those actions to which the body can be led, you will have life.
ROMANS 8:13

• •

Rules for proper behavior keep us from getting hurt. We risk our own life and the lives of others when we give in to our desires, whatever they might be.
LINDA BARTLETT

Sin

Some think that *sin* is too harsh a word. So they use euphemisms for sin such as *mistake, blunder, fault, offense,* or *violation,* which sound much better. We might try to power wash it, but sin is just that—sin.

The scriptures define *sin* as knowing to do good but not doing it. No one is blameless. We have all sinned and are in need of repentance and forgiveness.

Jesus came to fix the sin problem. Just ask Him. He's not afraid of the word *sin*—He conquered it!

If we live in the light as He is in the light, we share what we have in God with each other. And the blood of Jesus Christ, His Son, makes our lives clean from all sin.
1 John 1:7

"Come now, let us think about this together," says the Lord. "Even though your sins are bright red, they will be as white as snow. Even though they are dark red, they will be like wool."
Isaiah 1:18

"This is My blood of the New Way of Worship which is given for many. It is given so the sins of many can be forgiven."
Matthew 26:28

But He was hurt for our wrong-doing. He was crushed for our sins. He was punished so we would have peace. He was beaten so we would be healed. All of us like sheep have gone the wrong way. Each of us has turned to his own way. And the Lord has put on Him the sin of us all.
Isaiah 53:5–6

My dear children, I am writing this to you so you will not sin. But if anyone does sin, there is One Who will go between him and the Father. He is Jesus Christ, the One Who is right with God. He paid for our sins with His own blood. He did not pay for ours only, but for the sins of the whole world.
1 John 2:1–2

"All the early preachers spoke of this. Everyone who puts his trust in Christ will have his sins forgiven through His name."
Acts 10:43

What I say is true and all the world should receive it. Christ Jesus came into the world to save sinners from their sin and I am the worst sinner.
1 TIMOTHY 1:15

He carried our sins in His own body when He died on a cross. In doing this, we may be dead to sin and alive to all that is right and good. His wounds have healed you!
1 PETER 2:24

He has taken our sins from us as far as the east is from the west.
PSALM 103:12

We know that our old life, our old sinful self, was nailed to the cross with Christ. And so the power of sin that held us was destroyed. Sin is no longer our boss. When a man is dead, he is free from the power of sin.
ROMANS 6:6–7

He gave Him-self to die for our sins. He did this so we could be saved from this sinful world. This is what God wanted Him to do.
GALATIANS 1:4

• •

It is the very nature of sin to prevent man from meditating on spiritual things.
MARY MARTHA SHERWOOD

Sincerity

Sincerity is as welcoming as nestling in a cozy chair in front of a fire on a brisk, cold day.

The motives behind what we say or do are at the core of a sincere heart. Are our motives pure and genuine? Or do we possess a selfish, hidden agenda? Someone who demonstrates sincerity of heart and pure motives is a person whom we can trust.

Similarly, God expects us to approach Him in a straightforward manner with unadulterated sincerity. Hypocrisy has no place in our relationship with Him. God knows our heart and He seeks one seeped in sincerity.

How happy is the man whose sin the Lord does not hold
against him, and in whose spirit there is nothing false.
PSALM 32:2

No lie has come from their mouths. They are without blame.
REVELATION 14:5

Get your minds ready for good use. Keep awake. Set
your hope now and forever on the loving-favor to
be given you when Jesus Christ comes again.
1 PETER 1:13

Because we are men of the day, let us keep our minds
awake. Let us cover our chests with faith and love.
Let us cover our heads with the hope of being saved.
1 THESSALONIANS 5:8

As new babies want milk, you should want to drink
the pure milk which is God's Word so you will grow
up and be saved from the punishment of sin.
1 PETER 2:2

May God give loving-favor to all who love our Lord
Jesus Christ with a love that never gets weak.
EPHESIANS 6:24

We are not like others. They preach God's Word
to make money. We are men of truth and have
been sent by God. We speak God's Word with
Christ's power. All the time God sees us.
2 CORINTHIANS 2:17

"So fear the Lord. Serve Him in faith and truth.
Put away the gods your fathers served on the other
side of the river and in Egypt. Serve the Lord."
JOSHUA 24:14

You have made your souls pure by obeying the truth
through the Holy Spirit. This has given you a true love
for the Christians. Let it be a true love from the heart.
1 PETER 1:22

What will you do on the days set to have
a special supper for the Lord?
HOSEA 9:5

I am happy to say this. Whatever we did in this world,
and for sure when we were with you, we were honest
and had pure desires. We did not trust in human
wisdom. Our power came from God's loving-favor.
2 CORINTHIANS 1:12

You remember what we said to you was true. We had
no wrong desire in teaching you. We did not try to fool
you. God has allowed us to be trusted with the Good
News. Because of this, we preach it to please God, not
man. God tests and proves our hearts. You know we
never used smooth-sounding words. God knows we
never tried to get money from you by preaching.
1 THESSALONIANS 2:3–5

Bread with yeast in it is like being full of sin and
hate. Let us eat this supper together with bread that
has no yeast in it. This bread is pure and true.
1 CORINTHIANS 5:8

Put out of your life hate and lying. Do not pretend to be
someone you are not. Do not always want something someone else has. Do not say bad things about other people.
1 PETER 2:1

God has given me His loving-favor. This helps me write these things to you. I ask each one of you not to think more of himself than he should think. Instead, think in the right way toward yourself by the faith God has given you.
ROMANS 12:3

I pray that you will know what is the very best. I pray that you will be true and without blame until the day Christ comes again.
PHILIPPIANS 1:10

I am not saying that you must do this, but I have told you how others have helped. This is a way to prove how true your love is.
2 CORINTHIANS 8:8

• •

Speaking beautifully is little to the purpose unless one lives beautifully.
ELIZABETH PRENTISS

Sobriety

Sobriety includes several areas of behavior. Some scriptures refer to *soberness* as soundness of mind or exhibiting self-control. In other verses, *sobriety* addresses the negative influence of alcohol and intoxicants.

Either way, these passages direct us to be filled with God's Spirit rather than substances or attitudes that will control and destroy our lives. The damages intoxicants inflict are far-reaching, leading us into bondage. The scriptures warn us to flee from the things that have the potential to harm ourselves and others. So be sober, filled to overflowing with the Holy Spirit.

"He will be great in the sight of the Lord and will never drink wine or any strong drink. Even from his birth, he will be filled with the Holy Spirit."
LUKE 1:15

Wine makes people act in a foolish way. Strong drink starts fights. Whoever is fooled by it is not wise.
PROVERBS 20:1

It is bad for those who get up early in the morning to run after strong drink! It is bad for those who stay up late in the evening that they may get drunk!
ISAIAH 5:11

"They have drawn names to see who would get My people. They have traded a boy for a woman who sells the use of her body. And they have sold a girl for wine to drink."
JOEL 3:3

Who has trouble? Who has sorrow? Who is fighting? Who is complaining? Who is hurt without a reason? Who has eyes that have become red? Those who stay a long time over wine. Those who go to taste mixed wine. Do not look at wine when it is red, when it shines in the cup, when it is smooth in going down. In the end it bites like a snake. It stings like the bite of a snake with poison.
PROVERBS 23:29–32

"So be careful not to drink wine or strong drink. Do not eat anything that is unclean."
JUDGES 13:4

"It is bad for him who makes his neighbors drink, mixing in his poison to make them drunk, so he can look on their shame!"
HABAKKUK 2:15

"Watch yourselves! Do not let yourselves be loaded down with too much eating and strong drink. Do not be troubled with the cares of this life. If you do, that day will come on you without you knowing it."
LUKE 21:34

They are like thorns that tie themselves together, like those who are drunk with strong drink. They are destroyed like dry grass.
NAHUM 1:10

For the man who drinks too much or eats too much will become poor, and much sleep will dress a man in torn clothes.
PROVERBS 23:21

• •

"Abstain," says God. He doesn't say, "Be careful" or "Pray about it." He says, "Abstain! Run from it! Don't touch it! Have nothing to do with it!" Stay pure and blameless. If you don't, God will suffer most of all.
ANNE ORTLUND

Strength

Why do we wait until our strength is depleted before we seek God?

Women carry the weight of the world on their shoulders. We worry about our families as we manage our homes and assist our friends, churches, and communities. We maintain busy schedules as we transport kids to soccer practice and school functions. We cook, clean, work, and care for aging parents. No wonder we run out of steam!

Yet God wants us to rely upon His strength, not ours— to exchange our weakness for His power. What are you waiting for? Seek God's strength.

"For the eyes of the Lord move over all the earth so that He may give strength to those whose whole heart is given to Him. You have done a foolish thing. So from now on you will have wars."
2 CHRONICLES 16:9

"Both riches and honor come from You. You rule over all. Power and strength are in Your hand. The power is in Your hand to make great and to give strength to all."
1 CHRONICLES 29:12

This is the last thing I want to say:
Be strong with the Lord's strength.
EPHESIANS 6:10

We have been pure. We have known what to do. We have suffered long. We have been kind. The Holy Spirit has worked in us. We have had true love. We have spoken the truth. We have God's power. We have the sword of being right with God in the right hand and in the left hand.
2 CORINTHIANS 6:6–7

"He gives strength to the weak. And He gives power to him who has little strength."
ISAIAH 40:29

Wait for the Lord. Be strong. Let your heart be strong. Yes, wait for the Lord.
PSALM 27:14

The Lord will give strength to His people.
The Lord will give His people peace.
PSALM 29:11

"But the one who is right with God will hold to his way. And he who has clean hands will become stronger and stronger."
JOB 17:9

Then your lives will please the Lord. You will do every kind of good work, and you will know more about God. I pray that God's great power will make you strong, and that you will have joy as you wait and do not give up.
COLOSSIANS 1:10–11

O God, You are honored with fear as You come from Your holy place. The God of Israel Himself gives strength and power to His people. Honor and thanks be to God!
PSALM 68:35

He answered me, "I am all you need. I give you My loving-favor. My power works best in weak people." I am happy to be weak and have troubles so I can have Christ's power in me.
2 CORINTHIANS 12:9

• •

We must continue to ask God for wisdom and insight and for the strength to persevere. He will cause us to rise up and fly like eagles, walking and not fainting.
NORMA SMALLEY

Temptation

Jesus fasted and prayed in the wilderness for forty days and the devil tempted Him, albeit unsuccessfully.

Our Savior faced temptation, and so do we. Although it presents itself in different forms, temptation is what Satan uses to defeat, discourage, and pollute the believer's mind and heart. He will use every nasty trick and deceptive device to get us to sin.

But don't worry. Martin Luther once said that we can't stop a bird from flying over our heads, but we can prevent it from building a nest there. Temptation will come—but it need not set up housekeeping.

When you are tempted to do wrong, do not
say, "God is tempting me." God cannot be
tempted. He will never tempt anyone.
JAMES 1:13

"Do not let us be tempted, but keep us from sin.
Your nation is holy. You have power and
shining-greatness forever. Let it be so."
MATTHEW 6:13

But the Lord knows how to help men who are right
with God when they are tempted. He also knows how to
keep the sinners suffering for their wrong-doing until
the day they stand before God Who will judge them.
2 PETER 2:9

"Watch and pray so that you will not be tempted.
Man's spirit is willing, but the body does
not have the power to do it."
MATTHEW 26:41

You have never been tempted to sin in any different way
than other people. God is faithful. He will not allow you to be
tempted more than you can take. But when you are tempted,
He will make a way for you to keep from falling into sin.
1 CORINTHIANS 10:13

• •

Temptations come, as a general
rule, when they are sought.
MARGARET OLIPHANT

Truth

Your child gets in trouble at school. You question her, insisting on the whole truth. The doctor has bad news. You want the truth, despite your fear and hesitation.

In situations like these, truth becomes all-important. Yet truth is even more essential in our walk with God. In the Bible, the idea of *truth* carries four interpretations: 1) actual, true to fact; 2) real, ideal, genuine; 3) dealing faithfully or truly with others; and 4) truth in all its fullness and scope, as embodied in Jesus, showing sincerity and integrity of character.

To know Jesus is to know the truth.

Buy truth, and do not sell it. Get wisdom
and teaching and understanding.
PROVERBS 23:23

For the Lord is good. His loving-kindness lasts forever. And
He is faithful to all people and to all their children-to-come.
PSALM 100:5

"The Rock! His work is perfect. All His ways are right and fair.
A God Who is faithful and without sin, right and good is He."
DEUTERONOMY 32:4

Christian brothers, keep your minds thinking about whatever is true, whatever is respected, whatever is right,
whatever is pure, whatever can be loved, and whatever is well thought of. If there is anything good and
worth giving thanks for, think about these things.
PHILIPPIANS 4:8

"You will know the truth and the truth will make you free."
JOHN 8:32

"Anyone who has good things come to him in the
land will have good things come to him by the God of
truth. And he who makes a promise in the land will
promise by the God of truth. The troubles of the past
are forgotten, and are hidden from My eyes."
ISAIAH 65:16

Jesus said, "I am the Way and the Truth and the Life.
No one can go to the Father except by Me."
JOHN 14:6

For the Word of the Lord is right. He is faithful in all He does.
PSALM 33:4

"I set Myself apart to be holy for them.
Then they may be made holy by the truth."
JOHN 17:19

"These are the things you are to do: Speak
the truth to one another. Judge with truth
so there will be peace within your gates."
ZECHARIAH 8:16

The Law was given through Moses, but loving-
favor and truth came through Jesus Christ.
JOHN 1:17

• •

If we are Christians, we have committed ourselves
to the Lord Jesus Christ who said, "I am the Truth."
In giving ourselves to Him, we dedicate ourselves to
the truth not only about Him but about ourselves.
PAMELA HOOVER HEIM

Understanding

Eleanor Roosevelt said, "Understanding is a two-way street." We'd all like to be understood, but do we understand? To gain understanding we must consider another's perspective apart from our own. In essence, we must walk in their shoes.

Knowing God gives us a greater appreciation for and understanding of others. As we view people and life through His eyes, our viewpoint changes. The things we once questioned, we now perceive with greater clarity and purpose.

To understand rather than to be understood is every Christian woman's quest for spiritual maturity. To understand while seldom understood is that quest realized.

Happy is the man who finds wisdom, and the man who gets understanding. For it is better than getting silver and fine gold. She is worth more than stones of great worth. Nothing you can wish for compares with her.
PROVERBS 3:13–15

Then you will understand the fear of the Lord, and find what is known of God. ⁶ For the Lord gives wisdom. Much learning and understanding come from His mouth.
PROVERBS 2:5–6

They will not hurt or destroy in all My holy mountain. For the earth will be as full of much learning from the Lord as the seas are full of water. In that day the nations will turn to the One from the family of Jesse. He will be honored by the people as someone special to see. And His place of rest will be full of His shining-greatness.
ISAIAH 11:9–10

For wisdom will come into your heart. And much learning will be pleasing to your soul. Good thinking will keep you safe. Understanding will watch over you. You will be kept from the sinful man, and from the man who causes much trouble by what he says.
PROVERBS 2:10–12

Are you strong because you belong to Christ? Does His love comfort you? Do you have joy by being as one in sharing the Holy Spirit? Do you have loving-kindness and pity for each other? Then give me true joy by thinking the same thoughts. Keep having the same love. Be as one in thoughts and actions.
PHILIPPIANS 2:1–2

When I was a child, I spoke like a child. I thought like a child. I understood like a child. Now I am a man. I do not act like a child anymore.
1 CORINTHIANS 13:11

Wisdom is found on the lips of him who has understanding, but a stick is for the back of him who has no understanding.
PROVERBS 10:13

But You, O Lord, are a God full of love and pity. You are slow to anger and rich in loving-kindness and truth.
PSALM 86:15

"And He said to man, 'See, the fear of the Lord, that is wisdom. And to turn away from sin is understanding.'"
JOB 28:28

"Wisdom is with old men, and understanding with long life. With God are wisdom and strength. Wise words and understanding belong to Him."
JOB 12:12–13

Wisdom rests in the heart of one who has understanding, but what is in the heart of fools is made known.
PROVERBS 14:33

"But let him who speaks with pride speak about this, that he understands and knows Me, that I am the Lord who shows loving-kindness and does what is fair and right and good on earth. For I find joy in these things," says the Lord.
JEREMIAH 9:24

A foolish way is joy to him who has no wisdom,
but a man of understanding walks straight.
PROVERBS 15:21

An understanding mind gets much learning,
and the ear of the wise listens for much learning.
PROVERBS 18:15

If you have all these things and keep growing in them, they
will keep you from being of no use and from having no
fruit when it comes to knowing our Lord Jesus Christ.
2 PETER 1:8

Make me understand the way of Your Law
so I will talk about Your great works.
PSALM 119:27

The rich man is wise in his own eyes, but the poor
man who has understanding sees through him.
PROVERBS 28:11

Teach me what I should know to be right
and fair for I believe in Your Law.
PSALM 119:66

• •

Yearn to understand first and to
be understood second.
BECA LEWIS ALLEN

Wisdom

According to Webster's dictionary, *wisdom* is "the power of judging correctly, following the soundest course of action based on knowledge, experience, understanding and good judgment."

God is wisdom personified. His wisdom far exceeds our most impressive reaches of thought. The scriptures explain that "God's plan looked foolish to men, but it is wiser than the best plans of men" (1 Corinthians 1:25). God alone is the source of true wisdom. Accordingly, we should seek His wisdom and discernment in every decision we make. To do so is just plain wise.

So, kings, be wise. Listen, you rulers of the earth.
PSALM 2:10

He who obeys the king's law will have no trouble,
for a wise heart knows the right time and way.
ECCLESIASTES 8:5

Say to wisdom, "You are my sister."
Call understanding your special friend.
PROVERBS 7:4

Do not be foolish. Understand what the Lord wants you to do.
EPHESIANS 5:17

"Whoever hears these words of Mine and does them, will
be like a wise man who built his house on rock. The rain
came down. The water came up. The wind blew and hit the
house. The house did not fall because it was built on rock."
MATTHEW 7:24–25

He who hates his neighbor does not think well,
but a man of understanding keeps quiet.
PROVERBS 11:12

A wise man sees sin and hides himself, but the
foolish go on, and are punished for it.
PROVERBS 22:3

A wise man hides how much learning he has, but the
heart of fools makes known their foolish way.
PROVERBS 12:23

Good will come to the man who is ready to
give much, and fair in what he does.
PSALM 112:5

He who listens to the Word will find good, and happy is he who trusts in the Lord. The wise in heart will be called understanding. And to speak in a pleasing way helps people know what you say is right.
PROVERBS 16:20–21

Whoever is wise, let him understand these things and know them. For the ways of the Lord are right, and those who are right and good will follow them, but sinners will not follow them.
HOSEA 14:9

My son, listen to my words. Turn your ear to my sayings. Do not let them leave your eyes. Keep them in the center of your heart. For they are life to those who find them, and healing to their whole body.
PROVERBS 4:20–22

The teaching of the wise is a well of life, to save one from the nets of death. Good understanding wins favor, but the way of the sinful is hard.
PROVERBS 13:14–15

To get wisdom is much better than getting gold. To get understanding should be chosen instead of silver.
PROVERBS 16:16

"Strength and wisdom are with Him. Both the fool and the one who fools him belong to God. He takes wisdom away from leaders and makes fools of judges."
JOB 12:16–17

My son, eat honey, for it is good. Yes, the honey from the comb is sweet to your taste. Know that wisdom is like this to your soul. If you find it, there will be a future, and your hope will not be cut off.
PROVERBS 24:13–14

He will be for you what is sure and faithful for your times, with much saving power, wisdom and learning. The fear of the Lord is worth much.
ISAIAH 33:6

I will show you and teach you in the way you should go. I will tell you what to do with My eye upon you.
PSALM 32:8

If you do not have wisdom, ask God for it. He is always ready to give it to you and will never say you are wrong for asking.
JAMES 1:5

The one who is easy to fool believes everything, but the wise man looks where he goes.
PROVERBS 14:15

For wisdom keeps one from danger just as money keeps one from danger. But the good thing about much learning is that wisdom keeps alive those who have it.
ECCLESIASTES 7:12

Let the wise man think about these things. And may he think about the loving-kindness of the Lord.
PSALM 107:43

The person who thinks he knows all the answers still has a lot to learn.
1 CORINTHIANS 8:2

· ·

Learning is not attained by chance, it must be sought for with ardor and attended to with diligence.
ABIGAIL ADAMS

Zeal

What comes to mind when you hear the word *zeal*? Slobbering sports fans? Wild-eyed fanatics? For most of us, those images aren't terribly appealing.

But the Bible's picture of zeal is different. It's an image of commitment—of God to His people, and His people back to Him. Scriptural zeal is a beautiful thing, a strong desire to do right by God and His creation.

You can't go wrong being zealous for God. A passion for serving Him—by serving the people around you—doesn't make you a fanatic. It makes you like Jesus!

For the strong desire for Your house has burned me up.
And the bad things said about You have fallen on me.
PSALM 69:9

Whatever your hand finds to do, do it with all your
strength. For there is no work or planning or learning or
wisdom in the place of the dead where you are going.
ECCLESIASTES 9:10

Being right and good was His covering for His breast,
saving power was His headcovering, clothing of anger was
his covering, and His strong desires were like a coat.
ISAIAH 59:17

Since you want gifts from the Holy Spirit, ask for
those that will build up the whole church.
1 CORINTHIANS 14:12

"I speak strong words to those I love and I punish
them. Have a strong desire to please the Lord.
Be sorry for your sins and turn from them."
REVELATION 3:19

. . . .

Zeal will do more than knowledge.
WILLIAM HAZLITT

Experience Anew the
Beautiful Wisdom of God's Word

The Refreshingly Approachable
New Life Version of the Bible

The Bible can change your life—and the New Life™ Version makes scripture easier than ever to understand. Based on a limited vocabulary of approximately 1,200 words, the NLV clarifies difficult words and passages for better understanding. Looking for a fresh perspective on God's Word? These lovely Bibles are for you!

Hardback–Printed Cloth / $29.99